Pocket Guide t[…]

But[…]

of Great Br[…] Ireland

Richard Lewington

British Wildlife Publishing

To Alexandra Georgia Lewington

Acknowledgements
I would like to thank Martin Harvey for his help in the preparation of this book and my editors, Anne and Andrew Branson at British Wildlife Publishing, for their enthusiasm and guidance. The maps are based on information kindly supplied by Butterfly Conservation and the Biological Records Centre, and published in *The Millennium Atlas of Butterflies in Britain and Ireland*.

First published 2003 by
British Wildlife Publishing
Lower Barn, Rooks Farm
Rotherwick, Hook
Hampshire
RG27 9BG

ISBN 0 9531399 1 3

Colour separations by GWP, Kingsclere
Printed in Italy by Printer Trento, S.r.l.

Contents

Introduction	4
Conservation	5
The structure of a butterfly	6
The life cycle of a butterfly	7
The butterfly families	8
How to use this guide	11

Main descriptions

Skippers	12-27
Swallowtail	28-29
Whites and yellows	30-43
Hairstreaks, coppers and blues	44-73
Duke of Burgundy	74-75
Admirals, tortoiseshells and fritillaries	76-105
Browns	106-127
Extinct species and rare migrants	128-140
Day-flying moths	141-143

Further reading	143
Index	144

Introduction

Butterfly-watching is now a popular and enjoyable pastime for many people. As a result, new discoveries are still being made to add to the already considerable knowledge of Britain's butterflies. From the 18th century, through the days of the Victorian collectors when butterfly-collecting was at its peak, to the present day, much information on these insects has been recorded, and no other country's butterflies have been so thoroughly studied.

These days, photography has replaced the need to collect specimens, and many people who are keen on wildlife and photography spend much of their time building up collections of butterfly photographs. New information, even about common species, is still being acquired and even the novice can add to the overall picture by observing and recording butterflies. Sightings can be sent to organisations, such as Butterfly Conservation, which collate records. From this information and our observations, fluctuation in populations can be determined.

Before records can be made, however, it is necessary for the observer to be familiar with our butterflies so that a positive identification is achieved. Sadly, Britain and Ireland have very few butterflies compared with the rest of Europe – just 59 residents compared with 440 species on the Continent – but even so we have some species that are tricky to tell apart. The main aim of this book is to provide the clearest possible means of identification, with illustrations of the upper and undersides of every resident and migrant British species, together with their early stages. As well as all the British butterflies, a few well-known and common day-flying moths have been included, as these are often encountered in the countryside by butterfly recorders.

Opinions differ as to the relative merits of photographs and paintings for identifying butterflies. The variability of photography can lead to confusion, but the use of accurate artwork can pinpoint fine details and differences between similar species and so result in more accurate identification.

Conservation

The decline of Britain's butterflies throughout the last century, and particularly since the Second World War, has been dramatic and a cause for great concern, not only to naturalists but also to many people who can still remember the pleasure of seeing wildflower meadows dancing with butterflies. The all-too-familiar story of habitat destruction, agricultural intensification, pollution and the ever-increasing demands on land, has resulted in all forms of wildlife, not just butterflies, suffering.

The possible effects of climate change may also influence the future of our butterflies. While slightly higher temperatures may benefit some species, the unpredictability of weather patterns could have a detrimental effect on others, and the outlook for some of our northern species, such as the Mountain Ringlet, is uncertain. Some rare species with specific habitat requirements, such as the Swallowtail, have benefited once conservation organisations have discovered their exact needs and put into effect appropriate management. However, it is worrying that some of the commoner species, such as Wall and Small Copper, have declined for reasons that are unclear. It is, therefore, vital that a greater understanding of our butterflies is reached and the monitoring of their populations continues, so this information can be integrated into management strategies for their habitats.

Butterfly Conservation is the largest insect conservation charity in Europe, with 11,500 members and many volunteer branches throughout the UK. Its aim is the conservation of butterflies, moths and their habitats. Through its volunteers and staff, the Society runs conservation programmes on over 60 threatened species of butterflies and moths, organises national butterfly and moth recording and monitoring schemes and manages over 25 nature reserves. The Society welcomes all newcomers to butterfly watching and conservation who wish to participate in any of its activities.

Further information on how you can become involved and make a real contribution to helping and enjoying butterflies can be obtained from: Butterfly Conservation, Manor Yard, East Lulworth, Wareham, Dorset BH20 5QP; tel: 0870 7744309.
e-mail: info@butterfly-conservation.org
website: www.butterfly-conservation.org

The structure of a butterfly

Butterflies belong to the order of insects known as Lepidoptera, meaning 'scale wing', and it is the overlapping formation of these pigmented and reflective scales that give butterflies and moths their wonderful variety of colours which make them unique. The two pairs of membranous wings are attached to the thorax and are supported by a network of veins, which are inflated and hardened when the butterfly emerges from its chrysalis. The main parts of a butterfly's wings and body referred to in the species accounts are detailed below.

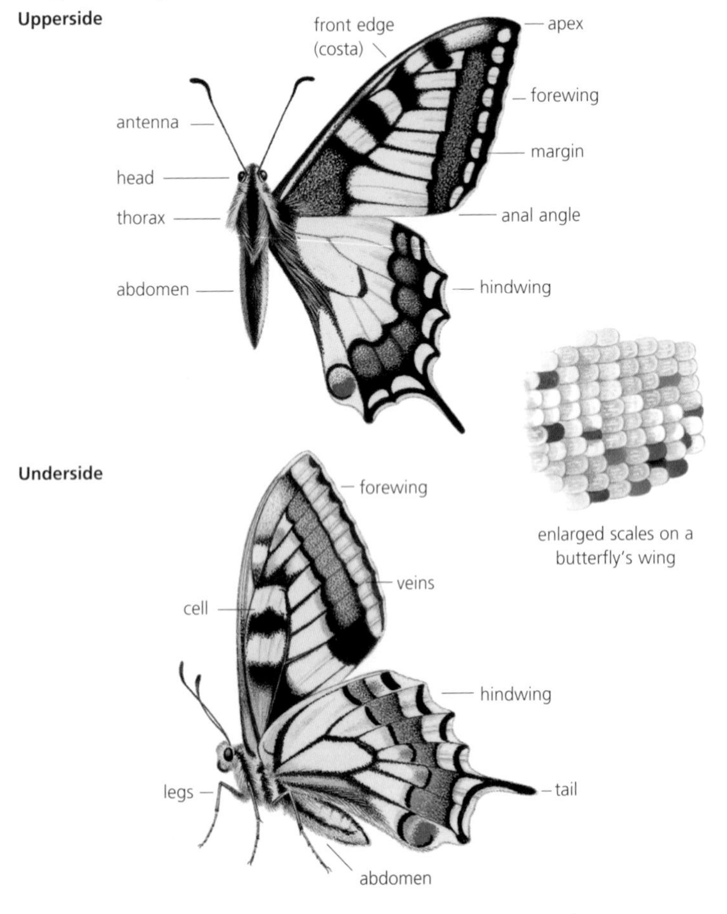

enlarged scales on a butterfly's wing

The life cycle of a butterfly

A butterfly has four stages in its life cycle. It starts as an egg, which may hatch after a few days or pass the entire winter with the tiny caterpillar formed inside. The caterpillar is the eating and growing stage, and can last from three weeks to more than 20 months in species which hibernate twice; this is the most familiar stage, after the adult. The chrysalis is the stage in which the greatest internal transition takes place, and often in just a few weeks a yellow liquid turns into a fully formed butterfly, which breaks out and expands its wings in preparation for a life which may last from just four days to 11 months.

Life cycle of a Peacock

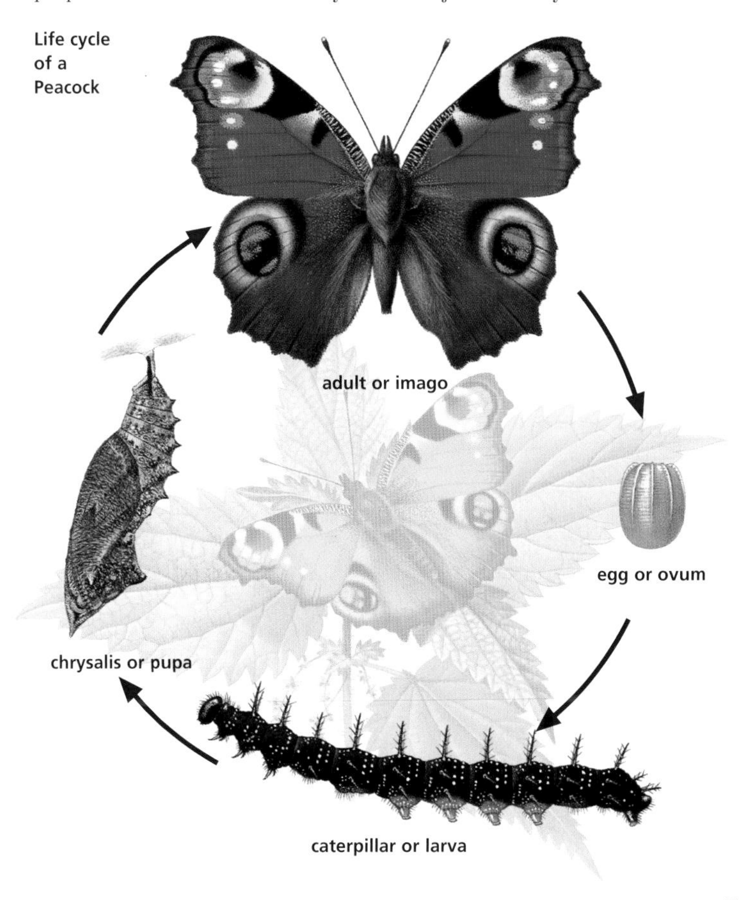

The butterfly families

These pages show a range of representatives of the five resident British butterfly families, and provide a quick reference guide to the main species accounts.

Hesperiidae – *Skippers* *Pages 12-27*

The skippers are often described as 'moth-like' owing to their small size, and relatively dull colours. Many skippers are predominantly a shade of orange, and some require close observation to identify correctly. They are easily overlooked but characterful butterflies, with a fast skipping or 'buzzing' flight.

Grizzled Skipper

Small Skipper

Chequered Skipper

Papilionidae – *Swallowtail* *Pages 28-29*

The Swallowtail is our only member of this splendid family, which includes some of the largest butterflies in the world.

Swallowtail

Pieridae – *Whites and yellows* *Pages 30-43*

The butterflies in this family are mostly quite large, with bright white or yellow wings. It includes the infamous 'cabbage white' (this name actually covers two species, the Large White and the Small White). The most familiar yellow 'white' is the Brimstone. Most whites have a rather 'flapping' flight pattern.

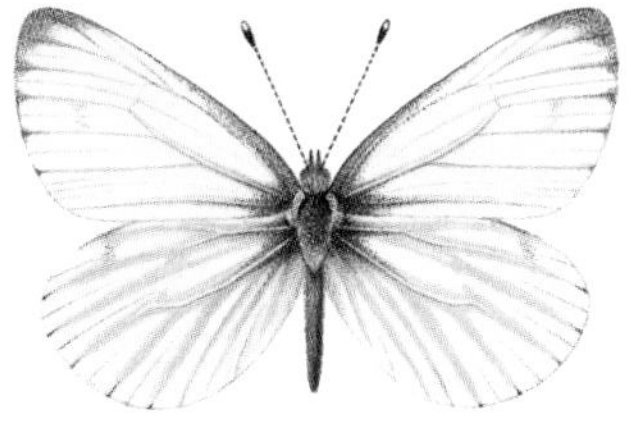

Green-veined White

Orange-tip

Clouded Yellow

Brimstone

Lycaenidae – *Hairstreaks, coppers, blues, metalmarks* *Pages 44-75*

The hairstreaks are quite small butterflies that spend most of their time in scrub or at the tops of trees, and can be hard to see. They are various colours, mostly dark, except for the brilliant green of the Green Hairstreak. Hairstreaks get their name from a thin white line on the underside of the wings. There are two British species of copper: the Small Copper is quite widespread, but the Large Copper is extinct. The blues are also fairly small butterflies, with blue wings, at least in the males – the situation is complicated by the fact that female 'blues' are often more brown than blue, and one species, the Brown Argus, is not blue at all!

Within the Lycaenidae is the Riodininae subfamily, the metalmarks, the rare Duke of Burgundy being the only British species. A brown and orange butterfly, the name 'metalmark' really only applies to the tropical members of this family.

Black Hairstreak

Small Copper

Common Blue

Duke of Burgundy

Nymphalidae – *Vanessids, fritillaries and browns* *Pages 76-127*

This large family includes some of our rarest species and some of our most familiar garden butterflies. Many are strong fliers, with a flapping flight interspersed with glides and swoops.

The vanessids include familiar residents such as the Peacock and Small Tortoiseshell, and migrants such as the Red Admiral and Painted Lady. All are large and colourful. The caterpillars of several species feed on nettle.

None of the fritillaries are common, and some are extremely rare. All are predominantly orange, with a network of darker markings forming the chequered pattern from which the name 'fritillary' is derived. Most are species of woodland, and thrived in woodland clearings when coppicing was the traditional way of managing woods. Fritillaries can be hard to identify accurately, and a good view of the underside of the wings is often needed for confirmation. They are sometimes confused with the Comma, a fairly common vanessid with similar colours.

The browns used to be given a family of their own, but are now considered a subfamily, the Satyrinae, of the Nymphalidae. Most are predominantly brown, but there is an exception, the Marbled White, which has a unique pattern of black and white. The browns do not usually display gliding flight. All browns feed on grasses as caterpillars, including woodland or hedgerow grasses. They are among the most numerous butterflies in a range of habitats.

Small Pearl-bordered Fritillary

Red Admiral

Small Tortoiseshell

Comma

Heath Fritillary

Marbled White
Speckled Wood
Scotch Argus
Meadow Brown
Wall
Small Heath

How to use this guide

The butterflies are arranged by families as described on these pages. All the illustrations of the butterflies and moths in this book are shown life size, and the early stages are magnified as indicated. Butterflies are depicted in typical, natural postures, as well as formal 'set' postures which show wing-shapes and markings to the full. For a few species, leader lines also highlight the main points of difference between similar species.

The maps show the general distribution of the species in Great Britain and Ireland (plus the Channel Islands). The life cycle charts indicate the usual range of dates for the various stages of the life cycle, but the extreme dates are likely to change with the prevailing weather conditions.

Plant names follow the *New Flora of the British Isles* (2nd edition, 1997) by C. Stace (Cambridge University Press).

Chequered Skipper

Carterocephalus palaemon

The brightest and prettiest of all the skippers, the Chequered Skipper now occurs only in western Scotland, around Fort William, where it was first discovered in 1939. The English population, which was centred around the east Midlands, became extinct in 1976, probably as a result of the widespread replacement of native woodlands with conifers, and the reduction in coppicing after the Second World War. Despite trial reintroductions in some of its former Lincolnshire sites there are, as yet, no self-sustaining English colonies.

The male is a typical skipper in his behaviour, darting rapidly to inspect intruders into his territory and spending much of his time basking on sunny vegetation. Beginning in mid-May, the flight period is short, lasting only until the end of June. Adults can be seen visiting spring flowers such as Bugle and Bluebell.

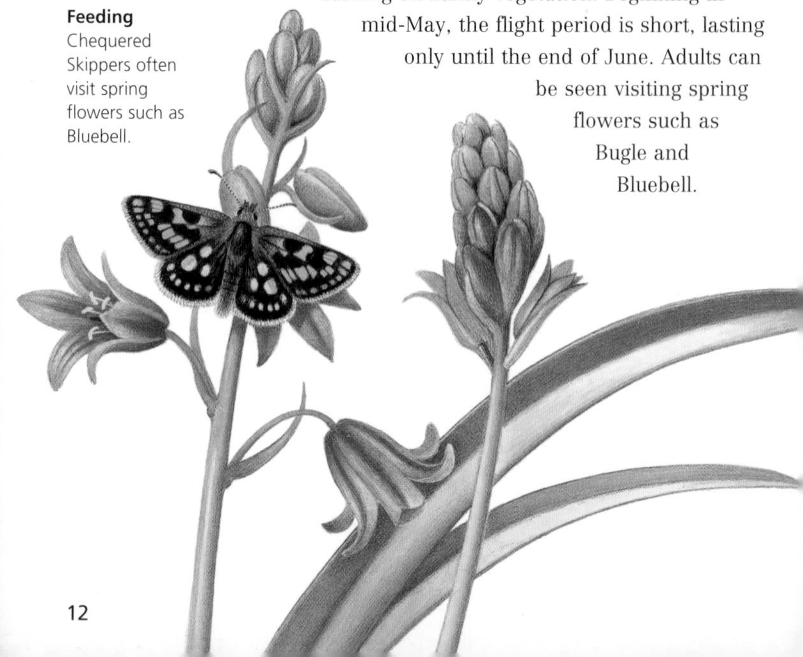

Feeding
Chequered Skippers often visit spring flowers such as Bluebell.

The Scottish population can be found along sheltered roadside verges, at woodland edges and beside some lochs where there are plenty of flowers, and where Purple Moor-grass dominates. English Chequered Skippers were found in overgrown woodland rides and clearings, and preferred False Brome as the larval foodplant.

Adult
The sexes are similar, although the female is usually larger, with paler markings. There may be some variation in the amount of yellow on the upperside.

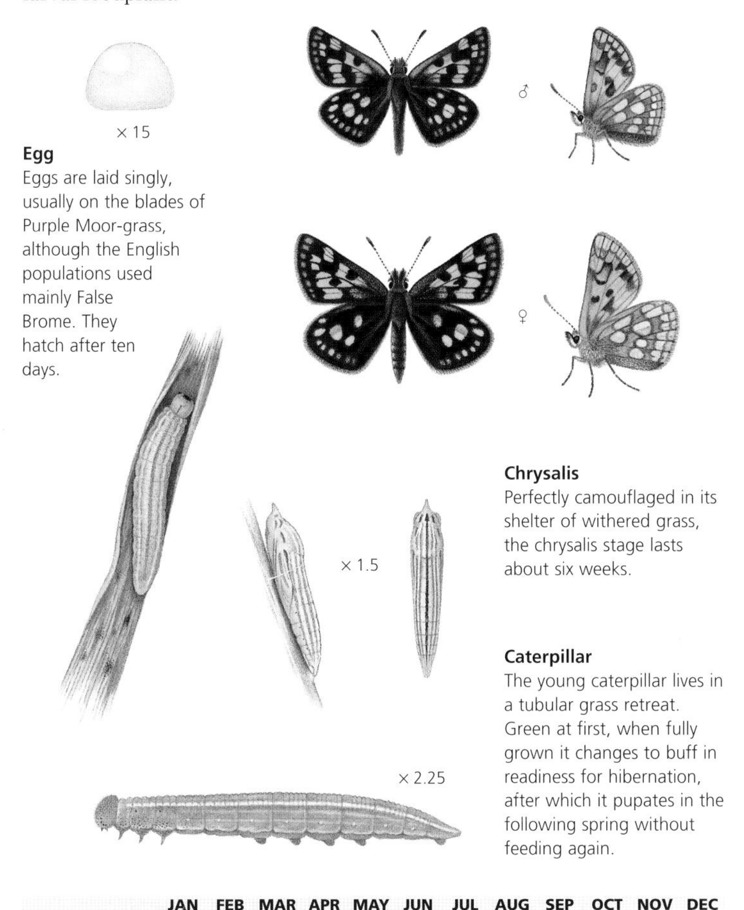

Egg
Eggs are laid singly, usually on the blades of Purple Moor-grass, although the English populations used mainly False Brome. They hatch after ten days.

Chrysalis
Perfectly camouflaged in its shelter of withered grass, the chrysalis stage lasts about six weeks.

Caterpillar
The young caterpillar lives in a tubular grass retreat. Green at first, when fully grown it changes to buff in readiness for hibernation, after which it pupates in the following spring without feeding again.

JAN FEB MAR APR MAY JUN JUL AUG SEP OCT NOV DEC
EGG
CATERPILLAR
CHRYSALIS
ADULT

Small Skipper

Thymelicus sylvestris

This is a common and lively little butterfly of southern and central England and Wales, whose range has expanded north as far as Northumberland in recent years. It is found on rough grassland, uncultivated hillsides, woodland edges, sea cliffs and downland, wherever there is an abundance of tall grasses, wild flowers and scrub.

Small Skippers appear in early June and fly until the beginning of September. They feed on a variety of wild flowers, with a preference for the purple knapweeds and thistles, and are often found in the company of other skippers, including the Essex Skipper, with which they may be confused. The best way of telling these two species apart is to look at them head on, to obtain a clear view of the undersides of the tips of the antennae. In the Small Skipper these are orange-brown, while in the Essex Skipper they are ink-black. The male Small Skipper also has longer, curved and more conspicuous sex brands (the black streak on each forewing). The other common skipper, the Large Skipper, may be found in similar places but is bigger, is brighter and has more variegated wing markings. The Lulworth Skipper is darker, with crescent-shaped markings, and is restricted to south Dorset.

Basking
Male and female on Yorkshire-fog, in typical skipper posture, with forewings swept back and hindwings held flat.

Although the abundance and the expansion in the range of this butterfly are reassuring, it should be remembered that the early stages of this and other skippers overwinter in the sheaths of longer grasses. Cutting can result in severe declines in numbers, as the tiny caterpillars are unable to drop to the ground, and leaving some areas of longer grass over winter will therefore be of benefit to breeding skippers.

Adult
The male has slightly curved, conspicuous sex brands. The female is plain orange, but the undersides of both sexes are similar, with little individual variation. The undersides of the tips of the antennae are orange-brown.

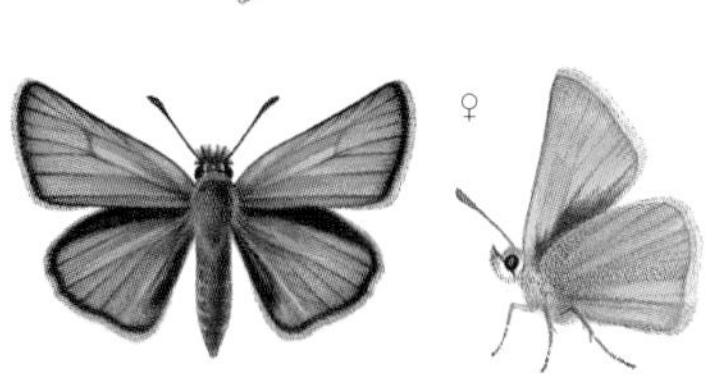

Egg
Laid in rows in the sheaths of Yorkshire-fog or Creeping Soft-grass, the eggs hatch after three weeks and the tiny caterpillars immediately spin little cocoons in which they hibernate together.

× 15

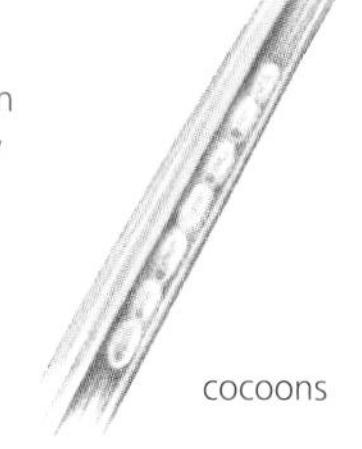
cocoons

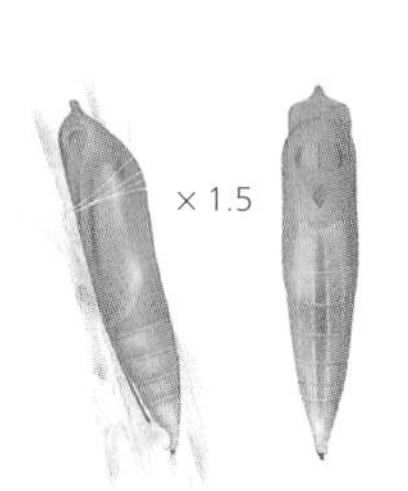
× 1.5

Caterpillar
This stage lasts for about ten months. The caterpillar emerges from its cocoon in April and makes a tubular shelter, which it enlarges as it grows.

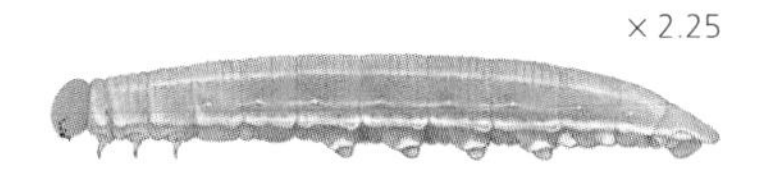
× 2.25

Chrysalis
Formed at the base of grasses, this is pale green with a short, pinkish beak, and is supported by a loose silken girdle. The butterfly emerges after about two weeks.

JAN FEB MAR APR MAY JUN JUL AUG SEP OCT NOV DEC

EGG
CATERPILLAR
CHRYSALIS
ADULT

Essex Skipper

Thymelicus lineola

Like the Small Skipper, this little butterfly has expanded its range considerably over the past 30 years, and is found in southern England from as far west as the Severn estuary, north to the Humber. Despite having first been caught in the 1820s, it was not recognised as a new species until 1889, in Essex, hence its common name.

The similarity with the Small Skipper still leads to confusion, as the two not only look alike but also share the same habitats and flight times. Usually, however, the Essex Skipper appears later, at the end of June, and continues until the end of August. The black tips to the undersides of the antennae are the best means of separation from the Small Skipper. For more detailed comparison with similar species, see Small Skipper.

Resting
Male and female Essex Skippers at rest on Salad Burnet.

Purple flowers are a favoured nectar source and Essex Skippers can be found in many warm, grassy places, from downland to roadside verges and overgrown sea walls. The female is less often encountered than the male but may be seen flying low among grasses, searching for suitable egg-laying sites. Its preference for longer grass makes it a successful coloniser of roadside verges, and good populations may be found alongside some motorways.

The present status of this butterfly is good and it is likely that its distribution will continue to expand.

Adult

The male has short, straight, inconspicuous sex brands. The female is plain orange, with the dark borders sometimes radiating along the veins. The undersides of both sexes are similar, being slightly more straw-coloured than the Small Skipper. The undersides of the tips of the antennae are black.

♂

♀

× 15

Chrysalis

Formed at the base of the foodplant, this is pale green with a white beak and tail. Adults emerge after about three weeks.

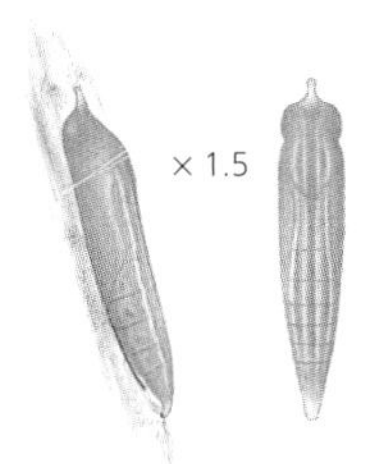

× 1.5

Egg

Laid in rows in the sheaths of various grasses, especially Cock's-foot, Creeping Soft-grass and Tor-grass, the eggs overwinter until the following April.

Caterpillar

On hatching in spring, the caterpillar spins together a blade of grass to form a tube in which it lives, emerging to feed. It differs from the Small Skipper in having a brown-striped head.

× 4.5

× 2.25

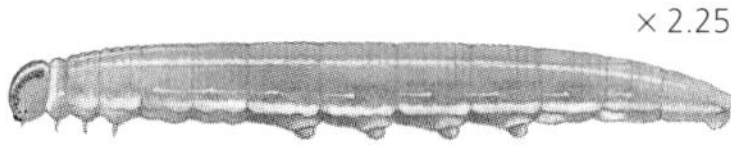

	JAN	FEB	MAR	APR	MAY	JUN	JUL	AUG	SEP	OCT	NOV	DEC
EGG												
CATERPILLAR												
CHRYSALIS												
ADULT												

Lulworth Skipper

Thymelicus acteon

Restricted to south-facing grassy hillsides and cliffs in south Dorset, this highly active little skipper, which was first discovered in 1832, is often abundant on hot summer days, when it buzzes from flower to flower, sparring with other skippers on the way. In Britain it is at the northernmost edge of its range and is seldom found further than five miles from the coast. However, this has not stopped it from thriving in suitable localities and, although the Lulworth Skipper has not expanded its distribution, it is as plentiful now as it has always been.

Unlike many butterflies of chalk and limestone grassland, the Lulworth Skipper prefers longer grasses, particularly where large tussocks of Tor-grass, the caterpillar's foodplant, grow among a mix of wild flowers such as Marjoram and thistles. Adults appear on the wing later than the other 'orange' skippers, flying from the end of June until mid-September, with sunny August days being the best time to see them.

♀ ♂

Resting
The male and female Lulworth Skipper perching on Tor-grass, the caterpillar's foodplant.

Many colonies are secure, either on army ranges or on steep slopes and coves that would be hard to plough or to be 'improved' with fertilisers, and where the grasses are allowed to grow tall. Here, many thousands of butterflies can be seen jostling with one another for nectar.

Adult
The smallest and darkest of the 'orange' skippers. The almost olive forewings have a crescent of rays; this is most obvious in the female, which is generally more boldly marked.

♂

♀

Egg
The eggs are laid in rows, tucked in the sheaths of the flower stems of Tor-grass. They hatch in two to three weeks, and the tiny caterpillars spin cocoons in which they overwinter until April.

× 22

Caterpillar
The caterpillar lives in a tube formed from the spun blades of Tor-grass, emerging at night to feed on the grass blade. The characteristic V-shaped notches of the feeding caterpillar are easily spotted. Viewed from the front, the caterpillar's head has two white, vertical lines.

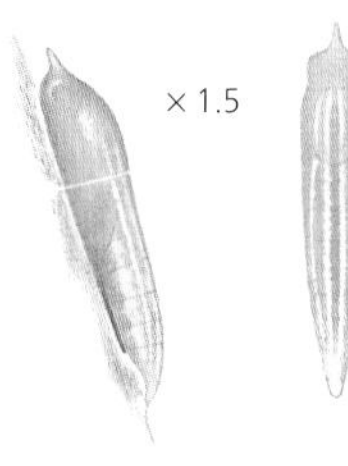

× 1.5

Chrysalis
This is similar to the Small Skipper, but with a longer beak and clearer stripes. It remains in this stage for about two weeks.

× 4.5

× 2.25

JAN FEB MAR APR MAY JUN JUL AUG SEP OCT NOV DEC

EGG
CATERPILLAR
CHRYSALIS
ADULT

Silver-spotted Skipper

Hesperia comma

A lover of warm, chalk downland, this skipper survives only if the flowery turf is short and broken, allowing the ground to become baked by the sun. In England, it is on the northern edge of its range and is not found further north than the Chilterns. It declined considerably in recent decades, although there has been a partial re-expansion since the 1980s and it has been found breeding in areas of longer turf than formerly.

It is on the wing in the peak summer months, first appearing in late July and lasting into mid-September. Where conditions are right, good numbers may occur, feeding on Dwarf Thistle, Marjoram and other downland plants and basking on chalky slopes. The dazzling speed of the male when sparring with other males, or during courtship, makes it difficult to follow in the summer sunshine. This contrasts with the cautious, discreet behaviour of the egg-laying female as she carefully selects a sheltered tussock of Sheep's-fescue on which to lay her large, bun-shaped eggs. There is

Basking
Male and female Silver-spotted Skippers spend much of their lives basking on the ground.

sometimes a slight overlap in the flight periods of the Silver-spotted Skipper and the Large Skipper, which it most closely resembles, but that species is more often found among lusher vegetation. However, the main differences are on the undersides of the wings, which in the Silver-spotted Skipper bear pearl-like markings. These show through from the underside, making the upperside more contrasting.

The future of this butterfly depends on careful management, with undergrazing and scrub invasion being the biggest threats. Myxomatosis has had a detrimental effect on hillsides that were once heavily grazed by rabbits.

Adult
The female is larger and darker and has more clearly defined markings than the male, who has a dark sex brand with a pale central streak on each forewing. The wings are narrower and more chequered than in the Large Skipper.

Egg
The large eggs are laid singly on straggly tussocks of Sheep's-fescue and are quite easy to find in the autumn. They overwinter, and hatch in the following spring.

× 1.5

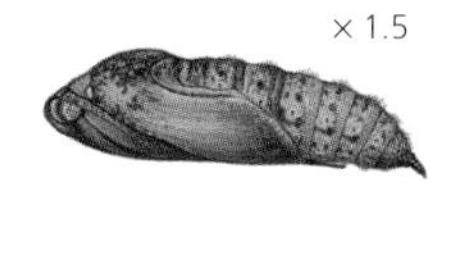

Chrysalis
Formed in July, in a robust cocoon near the ground, the chrysalis stage lasts for about two weeks.

Caterpillar
The restless, olive-grey caterpillar lives hidden in a tubular grassy retreat from which it reaches out to feed, drawing back quickly if disturbed.

× 1.5

	JAN	FEB	MAR	APR	MAY	JUN	JUL	AUG	SEP	OCT	NOV	DEC
EGG												
CATERPILLAR												
CHRYSALIS												
ADULT												

Large Skipper

Ochlodes venata

Our brightest and most widespread 'orange' skipper, the male Large Skipper is most often seen either perching alertly on sunlit vegetation in typical skipper pose, ready to confront passers-by, or dancing along woodland rides in the morning sunshine in search of a mate. Like the Small and Essex Skippers, it is expanding its range northwards, although it has suffered a reduction in its abundance in some parts of Britain, partly as a result of the general 'tidying-up' of rough grassy areas, roadside verges and field edges.

Single-brooded, the first Large Skippers are seen in late May or early June. They reach a peak in mid-July and have virtually disappeared by the end of August. They often fly in the company of Small and Essex Skippers, but appear brighter and more robust than these smaller relatives. The Silver-spotted Skipper is of a similar size but is a much rarer butterfly, found only on warm, south-facing

Resting
Male and female at rest on Cock's-foot, the caterpillar's main foodplant.

downland slopes, and has distinctive pearly patches on the underwings.

Fond of visiting wild flowers, Large Skippers also often come into gardens, where they feed on a variety of cultivated plants. The female spends much of her time resting in the sunshine, interrupting this with periods of egg-laying. She chooses large grass clumps on which to lay, curving her abdomen gently under a grass blade to lay a single pearl-like egg at a time.

Hibernation is spent as a caterpillar, hidden in a strong tubular cocoon made from grasses and silk. It is, therefore, important that not all tall grasses are cut at this vulnerable stage of the life cycle.

Adult
With bright golden upperside when fresh, the male has a conspicuous sex brand on the forewings. The female is usually a little larger, with clearer markings. The undersides of both sexes are a similar greenish orange.

× 15

Egg
The large, shiny eggs are laid singly on the underside of the blades of various grasses – usually Cock's-foot, but sometimes False Brome or Purple Moor-grass. They hatch in two to three weeks.

Caterpillar
This is similar in form to the Silver-spotted Skipper, but more blue-green and with a brown and cream striped head. This stage lasts for more than ten months, with the caterpillar hibernating part-way through.

× 1.5

Chrysalis
The dark, greenish-grey chrysalis is covered in a whitish, powdery bloom. It is formed in a loose cocoon, deep in a grassy tussock, where it remains for three weeks.

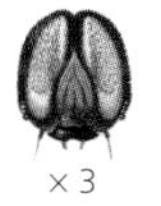

× 3

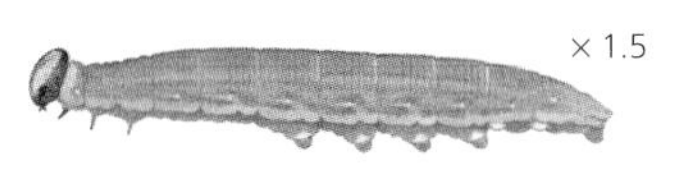

× 1.5

JAN FEB MAR APR MAY JUN JUL AUG SEP OCT NOV DEC

EGG
CATERPILLAR
CHRYSALIS
ADULT

Dingy Skipper

Erynnis tages

This active little skipper comes to life in the sunshine, buzzing low over the vegetation, often stopping to bask on bare ground. At night or at rest in dull weather it rests in a moth-like posture, unlike any other butterfly, with its wings wrapped around grass or flowerheads.

A local butterfly which has declined in recent years, it is nevertheless the most widely distributed of the skippers, being the only one to be found in Ireland, where subspecies *baynesi* is fully protected.

The Dingy Skipper is on the wing from late April until late June, and sometimes as a second brood in August. It may be found in a variety of habitats, including dunes, sea-cliffs, heathland and woodland glades, but the largest colonies occur on sunny, south-facing downland slopes. In any of these places it may be found in the company of the Grizzled Skipper, with which it is sometimes confused. However, its smaller relative has a more clearly chequered

Feeding
Common Bird's-foot-trefoil is most often used for egg-laying.

pattern, which is most obvious when at rest.

Some day-flying moths which fly in the same habitats and with similar flight periods may also confuse observers. The commonest of these are the Burnet Companion, Mother Shipton and Common Heath: they can be distinguished by their wing patterning and thread-like antennae (see pages 141-143).

Loss of habitat has resulted in local extinctions, and most remaining areas where the Dingy Skipper occurs require active management to prevent scrub invasion and the loss of Common Bird's-foot-trefoil, the caterpillar's main foodplant.

Adult
The sexes are similar, though the male has a fold of scent scales along the front of the forewings. The Irish subspecies *baynesi* has more clearly defined markings.

Irish subspecies *baynesi*

Egg
Laid singly on the leaves and stems of Common Bird's-foot-trefoil, but also on Greater Bird's-foot-trefoil and Horseshoe Vetch, the pale green eggs turn orange after about five days and hatch in around ten.

× 2.25

Chrysalis
Formed in the caterpillar's retreat, the chrysalis stage lasts for five to six weeks.

Caterpillar
The young caterpillar constructs a tent of leaves, which it enlarges as it grows. It hibernates in the autumn and pupates in spring, after ten months as a caterpillar.

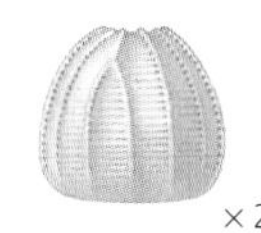
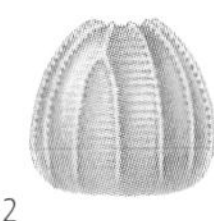
× 22

× 3

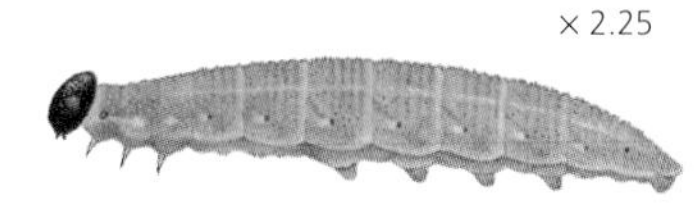
× 2.25

	JAN	FEB	MAR	APR	MAY	JUN	JUL	AUG	SEP	OCT	NOV	DEC
EGG												
CATERPILLAR												
CHRYSALIS												
ADULT												

Grizzled Skipper

Pyrgus malvae

The chequered, whirring wings of the Grizzled Skipper make it one of the hardest butterflies to follow on bright spring days, for it is an energetic, restless little insect and the smallest of all the skippers. It rarely visits flowers, and is easiest to identify basking in the morning sunshine, often on bare ground, when it can be distinguished from its near relative, the Dingy Skipper. In bad weather or in the cool of the evening, several may be found roosting communally on flowerheads, with their wings held tightly together over their backs.

Found in diverse habitats, including woodland rides, dunes, heaths and disused railway lines, it does best on warm, sheltered chalk downland, where it needs a mix of flowery vegetation and bare ground. The earliest

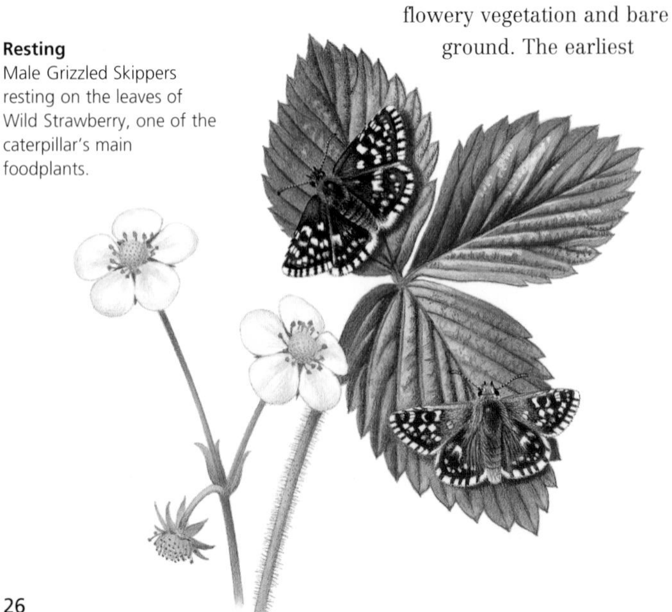

Resting
Male Grizzled Skippers resting on the leaves of Wild Strawberry, one of the caterpillar's main foodplants.

skipper to appear, the Grizzled Skipper sometimes flies as early as late March on warm spring days. The flight period continues into July, with an occasional second brood in August.

Like so many butterflies that require a short, mixed sward, created by grazing or rotational management of woodlands, the Grizzled Skipper has declined considerably since the 1950s. The largest populations are found in the southern counties of England, with smaller scattered colonies reaching into the north Midlands and north Wales, where it has become very scarce.

Adult

The male and female are alike, although the male is most often seen. Markings may vary, with extreme examples having the white spots enlarged, forming a confluent band. This is known as aberration *taras*.

aberration *taras*

× 15

Egg

The eggs are laid singly on a variety of plants, including Wild Strawberry, Bramble, Agrimony, Salad Burnet and Creeping Cinquefoil. They hatch in about ten days.

Chrysalis

Formed in a loose cocoon at the base of the foodplant, the chrysalis stage lasts throughout the winter, for about ten months, unless there is a second brood.

× 2.25

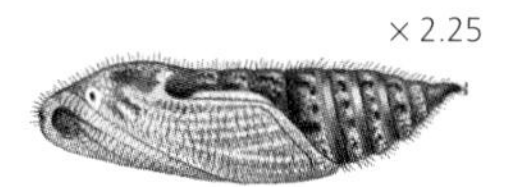

× 2.25

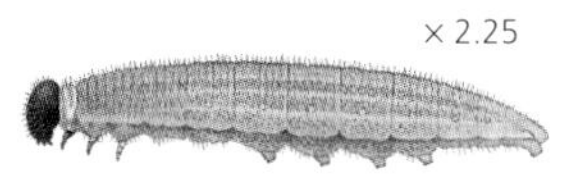

Caterpillar

The caterpillar lives in a tent of folded leaves, from which it emerges to feed. This stage lasts for about eight weeks.

JAN FEB MAR APR MAY JUN JUL AUG SEP OCT NOV DEC

EGG
CATERPILLAR
CHRYSALIS
ADULT

The decline of the Swallowtail during the last century was due mainly to the drainage of the fens and marshes of East Anglia. However, the remaining populations are holding their own, thanks to careful management which is aimed at clearing overgrown scrubby areas of fen.

Swallowtail

Papilio machaon

This magnificent butterfly, Britain's largest resident species, once occurred in marshlands throughout southern England but is now restricted to the open fenlands of Norfolk. Here it can be seen from May until early July, and occasionally again in August, flying powerfully over the Broadland vegetation, often appearing surprisingly well camouflaged considering its distinctive markings. No other British butterfly could be mistaken for the Swallowtail. Following the spectacular courtship displays, the female Swallowtail can be observed flying slowly, as she carefully searches for suitable Milk-parsley plants on which to lay her eggs.

The English population, race *P. m. britannicus*, is unique, and differs slightly from the paler Continental race, *P. m. gorganus*, which occasionally migrates to the downlands of southern England.

Feeding
Purple flowers such as Ragged-robin, thistles and even Buddleia are favourite nectar plants.

Adult
The sexes are similar, with little variation, although females are usually larger.

Chrysalis
Found low down on the stems of reeds and other vegetation, the chrysalis may be brown or green.

Egg
Laid singly, only on the leaves of Milk-parsley, the eggs are yellow at first but gradually darken. The caterpillar emerges after eight to ten days.

× 1.2

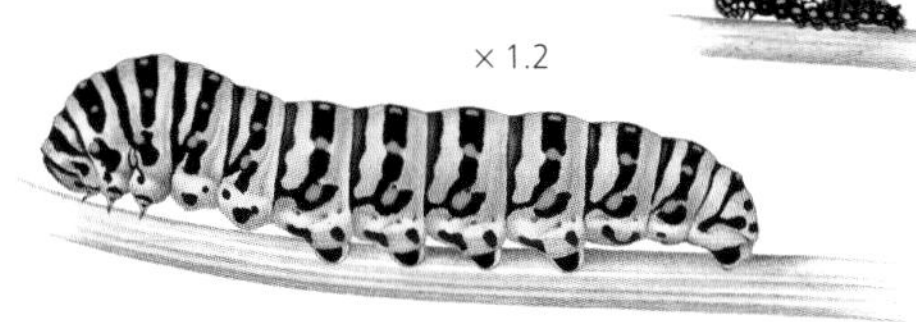

Caterpillar
Although resembling a bird dropping when young, the fully grown caterpillar is bright green with black bands spotted with orange. Despite the mature caterpillar's conspicuous warning coloration, it is still sometimes predated by birds.

	JAN	FEB	MAR	APR	MAY	JUN	JUL	AUG	SEP	OCT	NOV	DEC
EGG												
CATERPILLAR												
CHRYSALIS												
ADULT												

Wood White and Real's Wood White

Leptidea sinapis and *Leptidea reali*

In 2001, more than 110 years after the last native species of butterfly was discovered in the British Isles, a new species, the Real's Wood White, was announced. Its separation from the Wood White, which was first made in the French Pyrenees, confirmed that butterflies found in Ireland, apart from most of those in the Burren, were indeed of a new species. The differences, however, are minute, and are concerned mainly with the shape of the genitalia and the butterfly's DNA. Investigation of the physical and behavioural differences in the field continues to prove inconclusive, so the two species, which at the moment are separated by their distribution, are covered in this single account.

The delicate Wood White is the smallest and flimsiest of the whites. It is a local butterfly that occurs mainly along woodland rides, disused railway lines and scrubby undercliffs in the south-west of England. More recently, some of the best populations have been found around the edges of conifer plantations where vetchlings and trefoils abound. In Ireland, populations of Real's Wood White seem less restricted to these habitats and it may be seen along country lanes and hedgerows. Its flight is reportedly stronger than its British counterpart.

Egg-laying
The female carefully curves her abdomen to lay her egg on Bitter-vetch.

Two generations occur, the first in May and June and the second in July and August. Males of the second brood have smaller, blacker blotches on their wing tips, while in the females these are reduced or absent. This feature is, however, difficult to see in the living butterfly because, unlike the three commoner whites, the Wood White always settles with its wings closed over its back and never basks in the sun.

Populations of the Wood White fluctuate from season to season, but in England it has declined alarmingly throughout the last century, mainly as a result of the cessation of coppicing and the shading out of suitable habitats. It appears more stable in Ireland, which may suggest the wider presence of the more adaptable and successful Real's Wood White.

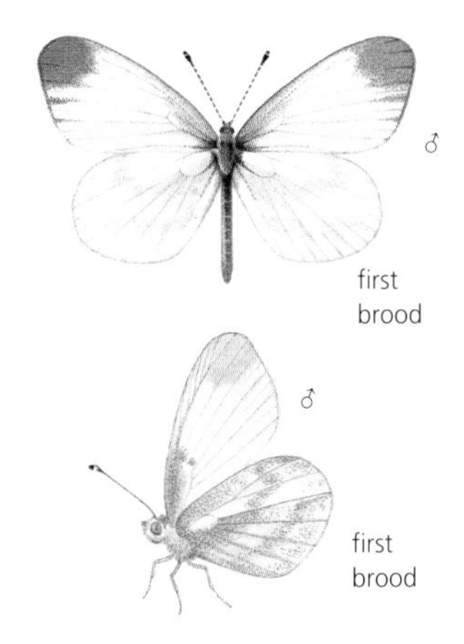

Adult
Males have darker wing blotches than females, blacker in the second generation. The forewings of females are broader. Irish specimens have attractive greenish undersides to the hindwings.

Egg
The elongated eggs are laid singly on a variety of leguminous plants, including Meadow Vetchling, Tuberous Pea, Bitter-vetch, Tufted Vetch and Greater Bird's-foot-trefoil. They hatch after about ten days.

× 15

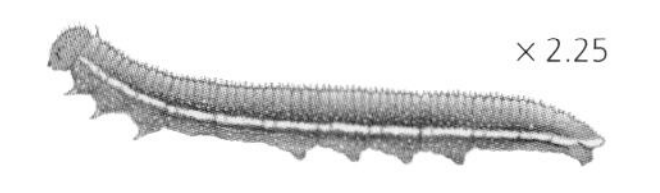

Caterpillar
After eating its eggshell, the beautifully camouflaged caterpillar feeds for a month, then leaves its foodplant to find a pupation site in taller grass or scrub.

Chrysalis
The elegant chrysalis, similar in shape to the Orange-tip, is secreted deep in vegetation where it is unlikely to be found. Hibernation is passed in this stage.

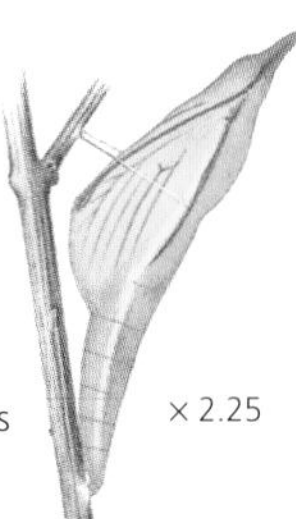

	JAN	FEB	MAR	APR	MAY	JUN	JUL	AUG	SEP	OCT	NOV	DEC
EGG												
CATERPILLAR												
CHRYSALIS												
ADULT												

Clouded Yellow

Colias croceus

A well-known but unpredictable migrant to Britain, the Clouded Yellow occasionally arrives in huge numbers, when golden clouds swarm along cliff-tops, gradually dispersing northwards. Most years, however, only a few arrive from the Continent, and are usually seen dashing across Lucerne or clover fields in late summer.

Nearly all Clouded Yellows arrive from southern Europe in the spring, although in recent years there has been some evidence of the successful overwintering of caterpillars. We are, therefore, dependent on the species' breeding success in North Africa and southern Europe to allow us the rare spectacle of a 'Clouded Yellow year'. Individuals lay their eggs on legumes as they roam the countryside, giving rise to greater numbers of locally bred butterflies later in the year.

Feeding
Male and female Clouded Yellows feeding on Red Clover.

♂

♂

Egg
Pearl-white when first laid, the egg soon turns pink then orange, and hatches after a week. Laid singly on legumes, mainly clovers and Lucerne but also Common Bird's-foot-trefoil.

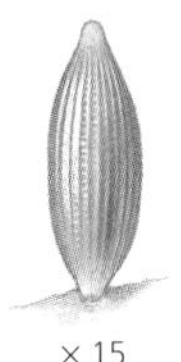

× 15

♀

♀

form *helice*

Adult
The male is distinctive – marigold-yellow, with solid black borders to the wings. The pale female form *helice* is heavily marked with black; this black marking is absent in the females of the rarer Pale and Berger's Clouded Yellows (see pages 128-129).

× 1.5

Chrysalis
This is well camouflaged, formed low down in vegetation near the ground. The adult emerges after about three weeks.

Caterpillar
Very like the Pale Clouded Yellow, which is slightly hairier and more granular-looking. It feeds for about a month.

× 1.5

JAN FEB MAR APR MAY JUN JUL AUG SEP OCT NOV DEC
EGG
CATERPILLAR
CHRYSALIS
ADULT

Brimstone

Gonepteryx rhamni

A welcome sight in the spring sunshine, the Brimstone is a wanderer in the countryside and may also be seen in urban habitats, wherever its caterpillar's foodplants grow. It is a long-lived, single-brooded butterfly, that first appears after hibernation in March or earlier. Mating takes place in the spring, after which some individuals continue to live on until July, with worn specimens sometimes overlapping those freshly emerged from the next generation.

In spring, yellow flowers such as Primroses and Daffodils are visited, but in autumn many Brimstones may gather in woodland rides, feeding on thistles, teasels and other purple blooms. They never sit with their wings open, and always hold them over their backs when feeding.

♂

Feeding
Thistles are a favourite nectar source in late summer.

The sulphur-yellow of the male Brimstone makes it one of our most conspicuous butterflies. The female is a pale greenish white and, despite the absence of black wing tips, is sometimes mistaken for the Large White. In dull weather and when hibernating a remarkable transformation occurs, and the scalloped, veined wings seem to disappear as the butterflies hang, perfectly camouflaged.

♂

Adult

Although the sexes differ greatly, there is little variation between individuals.

♀

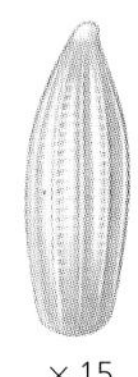

× 15

Egg

The eggs are laid singly on the young leaves of Alder Buckthorn and Buckthorn. They darken gradually, but are easy to find.

Caterpillar

The cryptically-coloured caterpillar rests exposed on the midrib of a leaf. It feeds for about a month before leaving its foodplant. It is easily found by first searching for leaf damage.

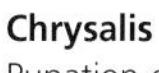

Chrysalis

Pupation often takes place well away from the foodplant, low down, beneath a leaf in tangled vegetation.

× 1.5

× 1.5

JAN FEB MAR APR MAY JUN JUL AUG SEP OCT NOV DEC

EGG

CATERPILLAR

CHRYSALIS

ADULT

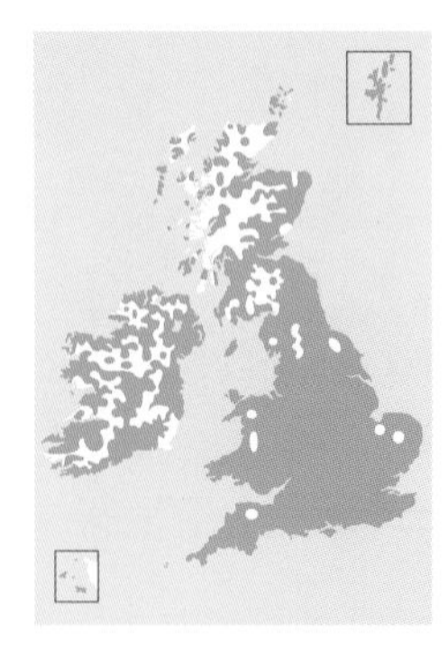

Large White

Pieris brassicae

Detested by gardeners, owing to the ravenous assaults of its caterpillars on brassicas and nasturtiums, the Large White is one of the few butterflies that can sometimes be classed as a pest. In most years its numbers are acceptable to all but the avid vegetable grower, but occasionally, as with other members of the family, its population can explode following mass immigration from mainland Europe.

Of the three common British whites, the Large White is the easiest to identify, as it is noticeably larger, with blacker wing tips and bolder spots, especially in the female.

As well as being found in town gardens, farmland and urban habitats, the Large White occurs in many other places, such as downland and woodland rides – in fact, almost anywhere.

Resting
Second-brood female Large Whites at rest on cabbage leaves.

Adult

The female has two bold spots on both surfaces of her forewings, whereas these are absent on the upperside of the male. Both have bold, black wing tips, especially prominent in females of the second brood.

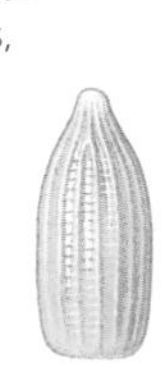

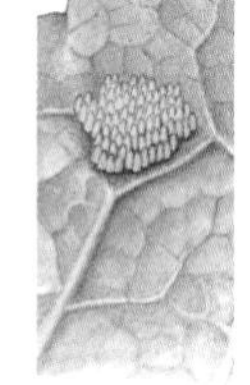

Egg

Batches of 40 to 100 eggs are laid, usually on the underside of leaves of brassicas, nasturtiums and Wild Mignonette. They hatch after about ten days.

Caterpillar

The conspicuous, smelly caterpillars contain mustard oils to deter predators, but many are parasitised by small wasps. They live gregariously, feeding in regiments for about a month. Occasionally caterpillars are found in the winter months.

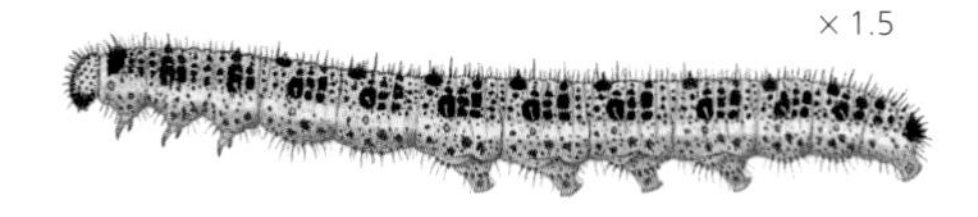

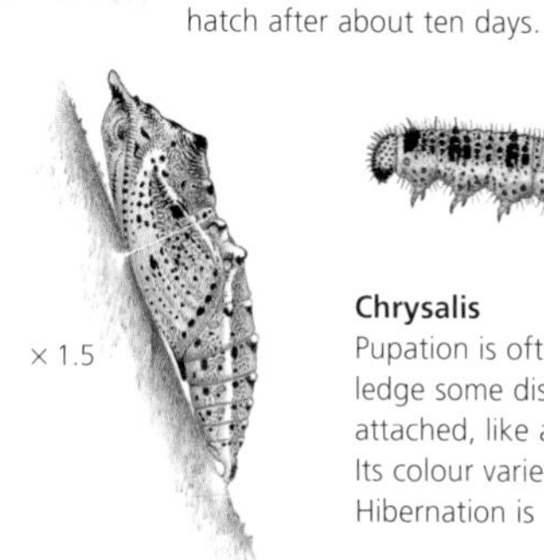

Chrysalis

Pupation is often on a wall, in a shed or under a window-ledge some distance from the foodplant. The chrysalis is attached, like all other whites, by a silken pad and girdle. Its colour varies, depending on its surroundings. Hibernation is spent in this stage.

	JAN	FEB	MAR	APR	MAY	JUN	JUL	AUG	SEP	OCT	NOV	DEC
EGG												
CATERPILLAR												
CHRYSALIS												
ADULT												

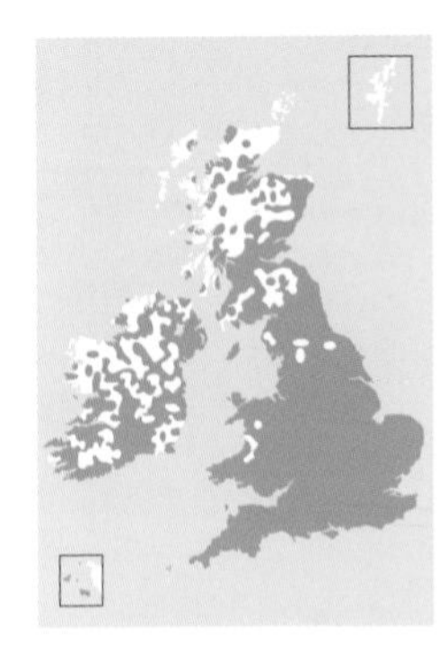

Small White

Pieris rapae

Disliked by gardeners almost as much as the Large White, this butterfly's caterpillars do not wreak the same havoc as those of their larger relative, as they are less voracious and lead solitary lives. Nevertheless, this is a common and successful species that is found almost everywhere apart from the far north, with reinforcements arriving each year from the Continent.

Its close relative, the Green-veined White, often causes confusion. The latter is also a frequent garden visitor, but the undersides of the hindwings show an attractive dusting of scales along the veins. The dark tips of the forewings offer the best way of differentiating the two species when seen from above. They

Feeding
First-brood Small Whites feeding from Dandelions in spring.

are pale and do not extend far down the wing in the Small White, whereas in the Green-veined White the grey veins darken at the margins, forming thickened triangles. The blacker, more clearly defined wing tips and the greater size of the Large White distinguish it, although occasionally large specimens of the second generation of the Small White may be almost as big.

Adult

The first brood males often lack the black spots on the upperside of the forewings. Both sexes of the second brood are usually larger and more heavily marked.

♂

first brood

first brood

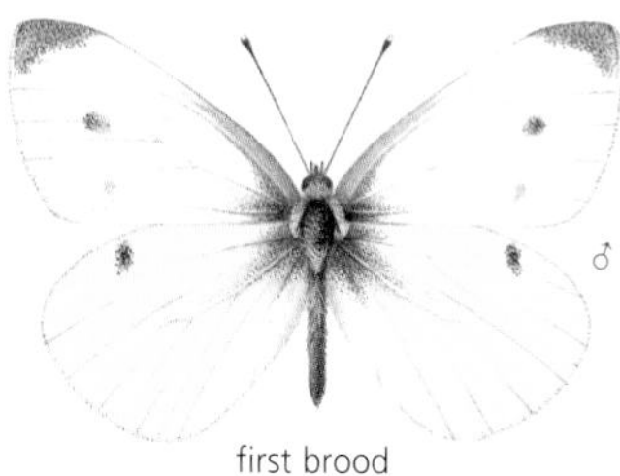

first brood

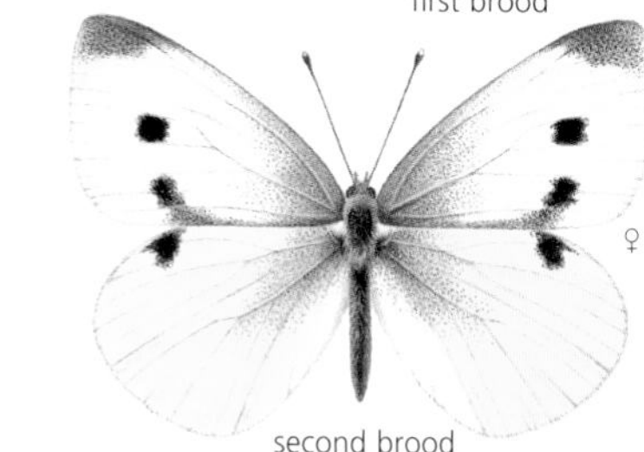

second brood

Egg

Eggs are laid singly on the underside of leaves of cultivated brassicas, nasturtiums and various wild crucifers, including Charlock and Garlic Mustard. Depending on temperature, they hatch after three to seven days.

× 15

Chrysalis

The chrysalis varies in colour from pale buff to green, depending on its situation. This may be on the foodplant or on a fence, tree trunk or wall. Hibernation, which lasts from six to eight months, is passed in this stage.

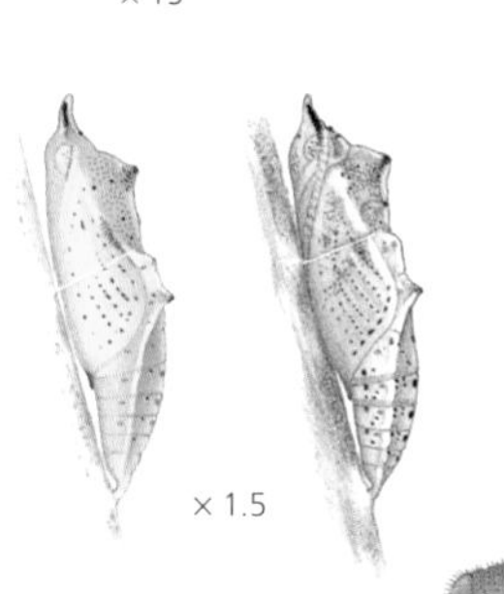

× 1.5

Caterpillar

The well-camouflaged caterpillar can be distinguished from that of the Green-veined White by the fine yellow dorsal stripe and the two yellow spots on the side of each segment. It feeds for about three weeks.

× 1.5

JAN FEB MAR APR MAY JUN JUL AUG SEP OCT NOV DEC

EGG
CATERPILLAR
CHRYSALIS
ADULT

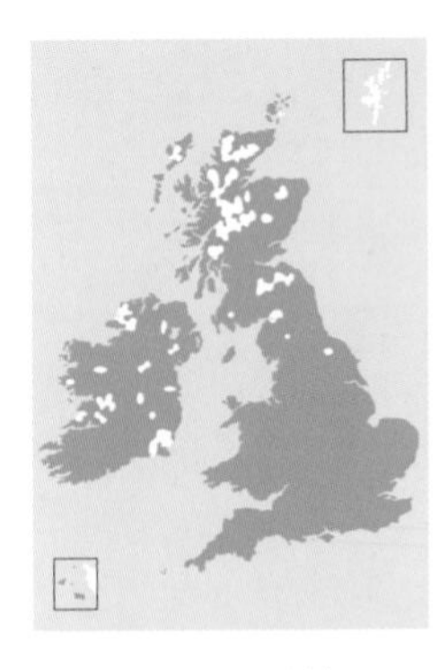

This is the most widely distributed of all the whites, being found throughout Great Britain and Ireland, including all the larger islands except Shetland.

Green-veined White

Pieris napi

Although the attractive Green-veined White is not a pest of cultivated vegetables, it can be just as numerous as its close relative the Small White. Though frequent in gardens, it tends to prefer slightly damper habitats than the other whites, being found in woodland rides, moist field margins and meadows. Further north, where it is more sedentary, it may be found on moorland and mountain slopes, where other whites are absent.

In flight it can be difficult to tell the two smaller whites apart. However, at rest the dusting along the veins, although sometimes faint, makes separation fairly easy. Small, poorly-marked males can sometimes be mistaken for the Wood White, but the latter is a much less widespread butterfly, which never stops to bask in the sunlight with its wings open.

One of the more variable of

Feeding

A variety of flowers, such as Garden Lavender, are visited for nectar. This is a male and female of the second brood.

♀

♂

British butterflies, the Green-veined White ranges from almost pure white with no black spots, to dusky buff heavily dusted with grey.

In warm years, up to three generations may appear between April and October.

Adult

Spring and summer broods vary, but the thickened triangles at the tips of the veins are present on all forewings.

♂

first brood

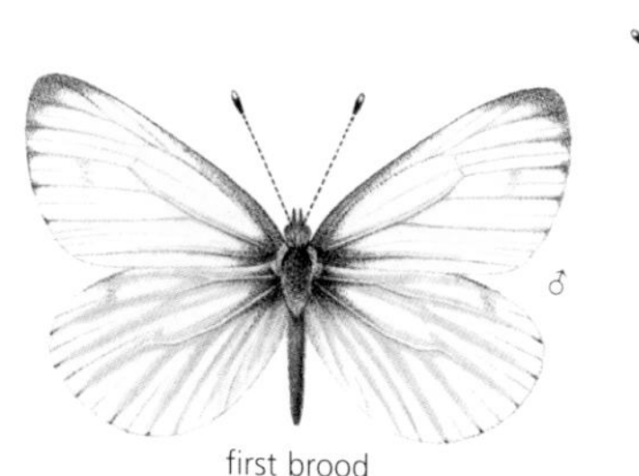

♂

first brood

♀

second brood

♀

first brood

× 15

Egg

These are laid singly on various crucifers, including Garlic Mustard, Cuckooflower, Charlock and Hedge Mustard. Nasturtiums and alyssums are sometimes used in gardens.

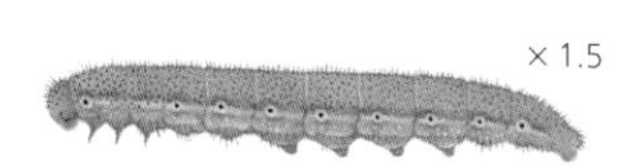

× 1.5

Caterpillar

This is distinguished from the Small White by the absence of a pale dorsal line and the yellow ringed spiracles. It feeds for up to three weeks.

Chrysalis

Variable in colour, depending on where it is placed, the chrysalis is shinier and less angular than the Small White. Those from the summer brood hibernate for about eight months.

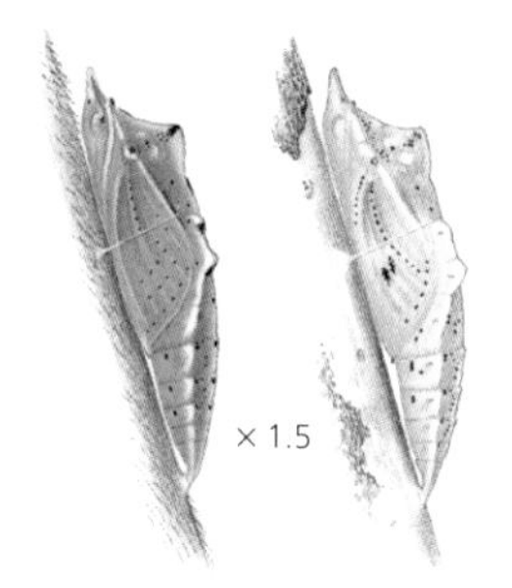

× 1.5

JAN FEB MAR APR MAY JUN JUL AUG SEP OCT NOV DEC

EGG

CATERPILLAR

CHRYSALIS

ADULT

A common, though rarely abundant species, the Orange-tip's range has fortunately expanded greatly in recent years, and after disappearing from Scotland about 100 years ago it has spread northwards once again and is more widely distributed now than ever before.

Orange-tip

Anthocharis cardamines

The first male Orange-tip of the year is always a welcome sight for butterfly enthusiasts. It is a charming little insect that wanders the countryside, along lanes, hedgerows, the edges of woods and gardens, feeding and searching the vegetation for females.

The female is more secretive and less conspicuous than the male. She lacks the orange wing tips, which warn of his unpalatability, and is often passed by as a Small or Green-veined White. However, she does share with the male the beautiful green-marbled underside of the hindwings, which acts as a camouflage when at rest on umbellifer flowerheads. From above, the female can be distinguished from other whites by the isolated black spot near the front edge of the forewings

Feeding
A male and female Orange-tip visiting Lesser Periwinkle in spring.

and the faint pattern showing through from the underside of the hindwings.

There is only one brood, with males emerging about a week before females, usually in April, and lasting until early July in suitable years. Further north, emergence may be two weeks later. Very occasionally, individuals are seen in August or September.

Chrysalis

The elegant, curved chrysalis is formed among vegetation, where it remains for ten to eleven months. Most are straw-coloured but a few retain the green coloration.

Egg

Eggs are laid singly beneath the calyx or on a stalk of Cuckooflower, Garlic Mustard or other crucifers in the wild. In gardens it is often found on Dame's-violet and Honesty. The egg turns bright orange after a few days and is one of the easiest butterfly eggs to find. It hatches after a week.

Adult

No other British butterfly could be confused with the male Orange-tip. The female is similar to other whites, and is best identified from the patterned underside.

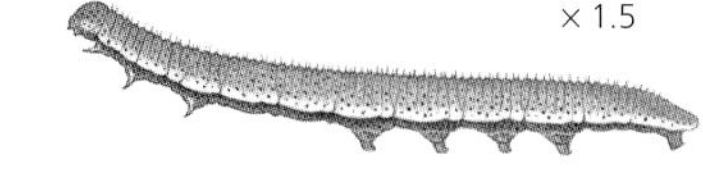

Caterpillar

The young caterpillar is cannibalistic. When fully grown it is perfectly camouflaged and rests and feeds on the developing seedpods, and less often on the buds, flowers and leaves. This stage lasts for about 25 days.

	JAN	FEB	MAR	APR	MAY	JUN	JUL	AUG	SEP	OCT	NOV	DEC
EGG												
CATERPILLAR												
CHRYSALIS												
ADULT												

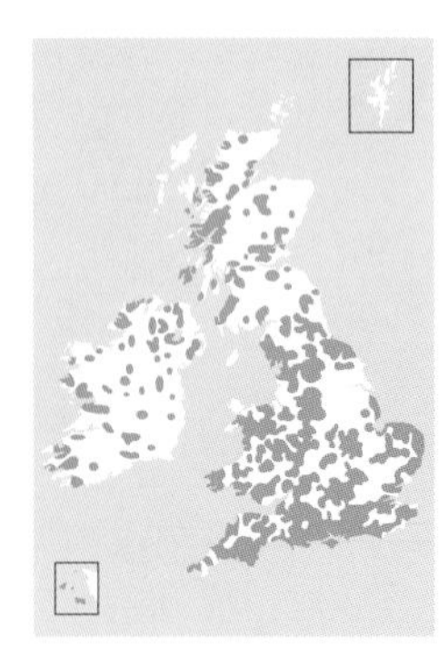

Green Hairstreak

Callophrys rubi

The smallest and most distinctive hairstreak, this little butterfly is the only British species with truly green coloration. It is also the commonest and most widespread of the hairstreaks, with colonies scattered throughout Britain and Ireland. Although it is found in a wide range of habitats, including chalk downland, moorland, scrubby hillsides and disused railway lines, it does best on heathland where it may be abundant. The main requirements for this sedentary butterfly are warm open areas with some scrub, sheltered from the wind by a mix of larger shrubs. In recent years, many suitable habitats have been destroyed or have become overgrown and, although new colonies are still being discovered, the Green Hairstreak has declined in some regions. Colonies are sometimes discovered by chance on country walks, when individuals are accidentally disturbed from the foliage.

It is an inconspicuous butterfly which is often overlooked, the male spending most of his life perching on vegetation guarding his territory and darting out to inspect rivals or passing females. The female is even less often seen, although she can sometimes be observed fluttering or crawling over the

Resting
Male Green Hairstreak holding territory on Gorse.

foodplant, carefully probing her abdomen into tender leaf buds to lay her eggs. The brown uppersides of both sexes are rarely seen as this butterfly always settles with its wings firmly closed.

The Green Hairstreak is the only hairstreak that overwinters in the chrysalis stage, making it the first one to appear in spring, usually in late April. It is single-brooded, with worn specimens sometimes lasting into July.

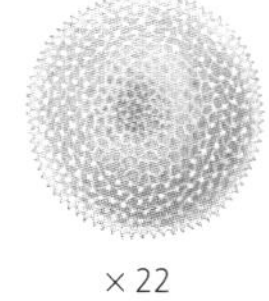

× 22

Egg
The soft, pale eggs are squeezed into the tender buds or shoots of a variety of plants, including Gorse, Bilberry, Broom, Dogwood, Buckthorn, Common Rock-rose, Dyer's Greenweed and Common Bird's-foot-trefoil.

Chrysalis
Formed on the ground among mosses and leaves in association with ants. It remains in this stage for about ten months, throughout the winter – the only hairstreak to hibernate as a chrysalis.

× 2.25

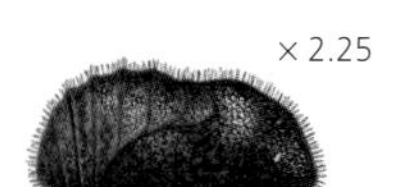

Adult
The sexes are similar, apart from a pale sex brand on the forewings of the male. The row of white 'hairstreaks' on the underside may be reduced to a few spots or may be completely absent.

Caterpillar
When young, the caterpillars are cannibalistic. They become beautifully camouflaged when fully grown and feed for about 25 days.

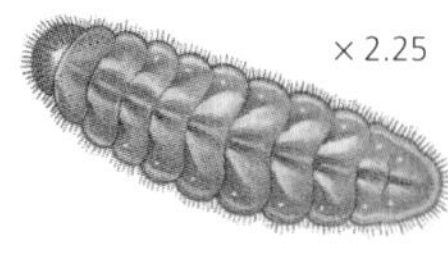

× 2.25

	JAN	FEB	MAR	APR	MAY	JUN	JUL	AUG	SEP	OCT	NOV	DEC
EGG												
CATERPILLAR												
CHRYSALIS												
ADULT												

Brown Hairstreak

Thecla betulae

Like most of the hairstreaks, the Brown Hairstreak is an elusive butterfly that spends most of its life high in the treetops, basking and feeding on aphid honeydew. Males congregate in the canopy of a favoured large Ash tree, known as a 'master tree', to await the females. Only on warm sunny days, after mating, does the female descend to lay her eggs, and it is then that she is most likely to be observed. Egg-laying usually takes place low down, among small, unkempt Blackthorn bushes growing in sunny, sheltered positions. Males only rarely descend to feed, but females intersperse egg-laying with visits to feed on the flowers of Bramble, thistles and Hemp-agrimony, when they are easily approached. The Brown Hairstreak is on the wing late in the year, from late July until the end of September.

The removal of over half of Britain's hedgerows in the past 60 years has resulted in the widespread loss of colonies, particularly in the east.

Resting
Female Brown Hairstreaks on Blackthorn, the larval foodplant.

The species is found in rambling colonies, mainly in southern and western Britain and western Ireland and, although it still occurs in some Midland counties of England, it has declined in many areas, especially in the east. In Britain, woodland edges, scrubby thickets and hedgerows growing on heavy clay support colonies. In the Burren and western Ireland they are found in lighter, limestone districts.

Adult
There is a distinct difference between the sexes, the female having a golden orange band across the forewings. The undersides are similar, but slightly bolder in the female.

Egg
Laid singly, but several may be found together. Searching for the eggs on the underside of Blackthorn twigs where new growth meets old is often the best way to establish the butterfly's presence.

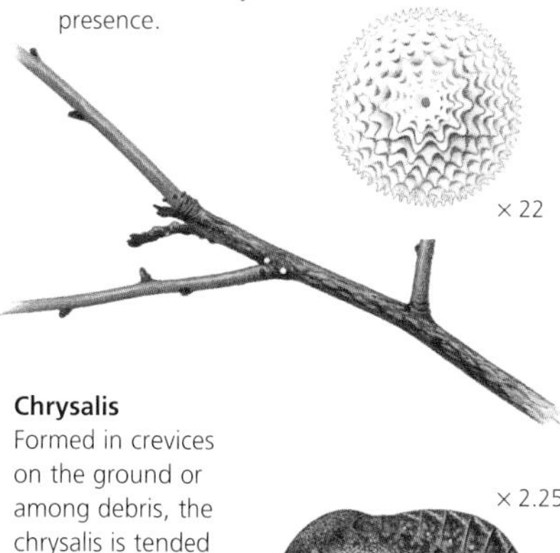

Chrysalis
Formed in crevices on the ground or among debris, the chrysalis is tended by ants.

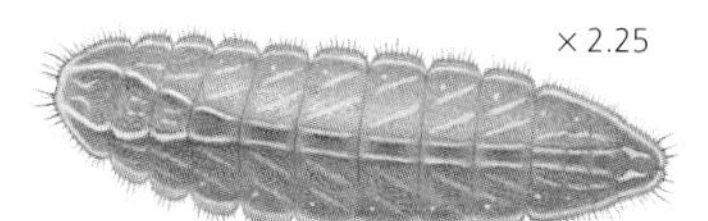

Caterpillar
The sedentary caterpillar rests beneath leaves in the daytime. It feeds and grows slowly for between seven and ten weeks, then turns pinkish before pupation.

	JAN	FEB	MAR	APR	MAY	JUN	JUL	AUG	SEP	OCT	NOV	DEC
EGG												
CATERPILLAR												
CHRYSALIS												
ADULT												

Purple Hairstreak

Neozephyrus quercus

Small, dark butterflies fidgeting around the canopy of mature oak trees are most likely to be Purple Hairstreaks. They can also be seen on large Ash trees, but the Purple Hairstreak is the only British butterfly that is reliant solely on oak to complete its life cycle. The adult is fond of honeydew produced by aphids high up in the trees, and is not often attracted to flowers, so rarely descends to ground level. Unusually for hairstreaks, this species basks in the sun with its wings open – the only hairstreak, other than the Brown, that does this.

The Purple Hairstreak is a lovely insect, with eye-catching flashes of purple on the upper surface of the wings. It is common in oak woodlands throughout Britain, but may also be found on isolated oaks in hedgerows or in

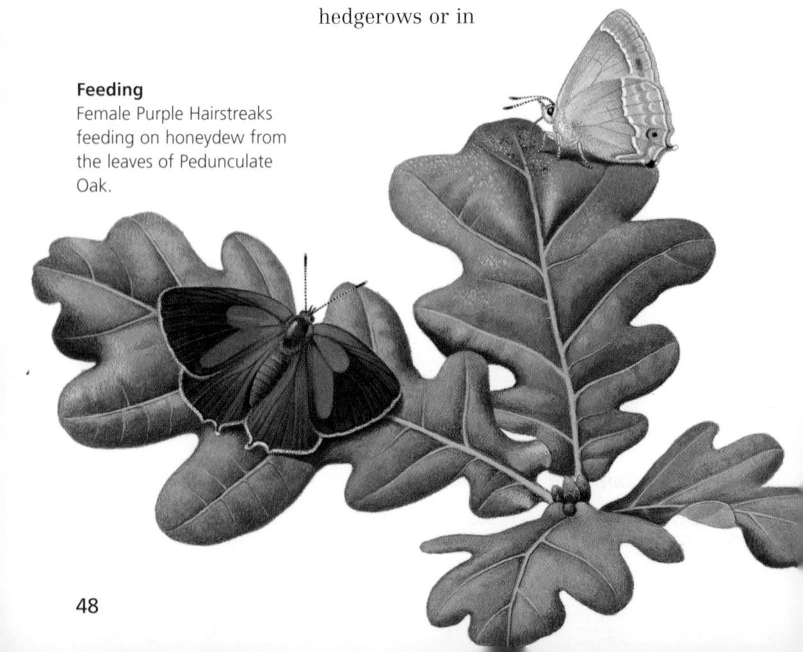

Feeding
Female Purple Hairstreaks feeding on honeydew from the leaves of Pedunculate Oak.

gardens. In Ireland, however, it is much rarer, although it is probably much under-recorded because of its secretive habits.

Purple Hairstreaks have one generation a year and fly from late June until early September. They live in self-contained colonies. Populations fluctuate greatly from year to year, and there can be occasional explosions in numbers when thousands may appear on late summer afternoons or evenings, providing one of the best opportunities to see these elusive butterflies.

Although this butterfly is doing well, with an expanding distribution, it is vulnerable to the loss of oak trees in hedgerows and the replacement of broadleaved woodland by conifer plantations.

Adult
The female, which is more frequently seen, is most attractive, with a bold purple patch on the forewings. The silvery undersides of both sexes are similar.

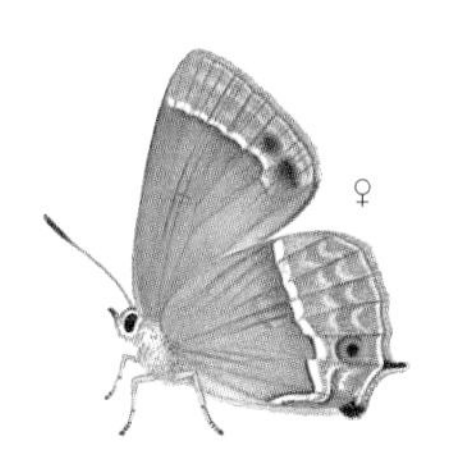

× 22

Egg
The eggs are laid singly at the base of an oak leaf-bud, and are fairly easy to find after the leaves have dropped. The small caterpillar remains inside the egg until the following spring.

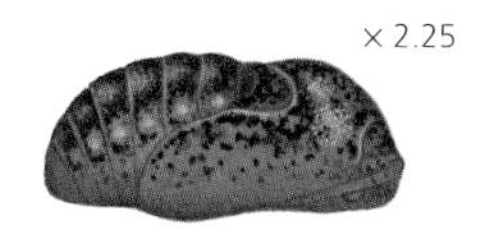
× 2.25

Chrysalis
The chrysalis is able to produce a squeak, which is thought to attract ants. It is formed on or under the ground, often in association with ant nests.

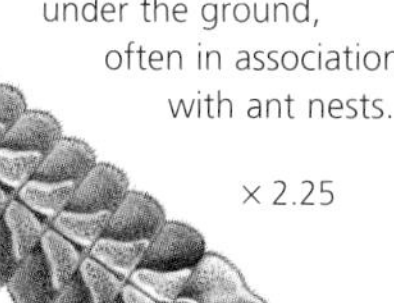
× 2.25

Caterpillar
Perfectly camouflaged, concealed among the scales of the oak buds, the caterpillar stage lasts for six to seven weeks.

	JAN	FEB	MAR	APR	MAY	JUN	JUL	AUG	SEP	OCT	NOV	DEC
EGG												
CATERPILLAR												
CHRYSALIS												
ADULT												

White-letter Hairstreak

Satyrium w-album

Disaster struck the White-letter Hairstreak in the 1970s, when Dutch Elm Disease decimated millions of Britain's elm trees, for the caterpillars of this secretive little butterfly feed exclusively on the leaves of various species of elm. Fortunately, it has been found that caterpillars can survive on new sucker regrowth, as well as the fully mature trees, and populations have now recovered in many places. Recently, the range of this butterfly has been expanding northwards, possibly as a result of climate change.

The White-letter Hairstreak has a fairly short flight period, with butterflies appearing throughout July until mid-August. Like most other hairstreaks, it feeds on honeydew in the canopy of large trees, although it may also be seen feeding from the flowers of thistles, Hemp-agrimony and Bramble.

It is the darkest and

Feeding
Creeping Thistles are often visited by White-letter Hairstreaks.

plainest of the hairstreaks, although the uppersides are never seen in the field as it always feeds and rests with its wings closed. It most closely resembles its near relative, the Black Hairstreak, but that has a brighter band of orange, with diminishing black spots, and lacks the conspicuous white 'W' on the hindwing underside.

Despite its misfortunes in the second half of the last century, the White-letter Hairstreak appears to be recovering well, although it has probably received more attention recently from concerned naturalists, and colonies are now probably easier to find in the suckering elms than in mature trees. There is, however, still cause for concern, as hedgerows of elm suckers succumb to the tidying up of the countryside, possibly resulting in populations becoming more isolated.

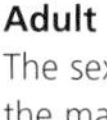

Adult
The sexes are similar, but the male has a pale sex brand on the upperside of the forewings. When feeding or at rest, the longer tails of the female are the best way to tell the sexes apart.

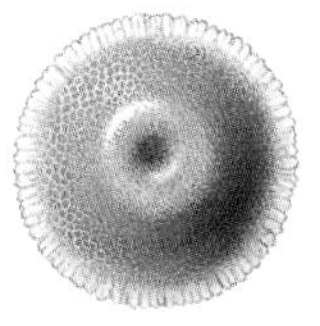
× 22

Egg
The button-shaped eggs are laid in the fork of an elm twig. They gradually darken with age and hatch in March or April, having overwintered for eight months.

Chrysalis
Formed on elm leaves or twigs, it looks just like a brown scaly bud. The butterfly emerges after three to four weeks.

× 2.25

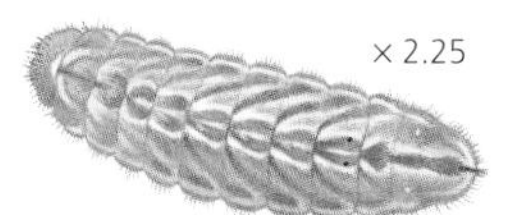
× 2.25

Caterpillar
The caterpillar feeds on the buds and leaves of elm, and when fully grown at six weeks its cryptic markings closely resemble the texture of the leaves.

	JAN	FEB	MAR	APR	MAY	JUN	JUL	AUG	SEP	OCT	NOV	DEC
EGG												
CATERPILLAR												
CHRYSALIS												
ADULT												

Black Hairstreak

Satyrium pruni

The Black Hairstreak is a local, sedentary butterfly, with a distribution which is restricted to around 45 colonies in the south and east Midlands. It has a short flight period, from mid-June to mid-July, making it an elusive and enigmatic little butterfly. It is found in sunny woodland glades and edges, where large mature stands of Blackthorn grow, sheltered from the wind. Much of its time is spent feeding on honeydew in the tops of larger trees. The flowers of Wild Privet and Way-faring Tree may also be visited for nectar. Early afternoon is the best time to search for this species, when butterflies are easier to approach and photograph.

Care should be taken when identifying this hairstreak, as both the White-lettered and the Purple Hairstreak have a similar jerky flight and may fly together with the Black, all three being difficult to separate high in the canopy. As the uppersides are rarely seen, the bright orange band on the hindwings, with tapering black dots, is its best distinguishing feature. Binoculars make the task easier.

Resting
Black Hairstreak perching on a leaf of Blackthorn.

The Black Hairstreak declined at the beginning of the last century as a result of loss of habitat and changes in woodland management. Its status is now fairly stable, although numbers of adults may vary greatly from year to year. More recently, the increase in deer populations in the woods of southern Britain has posed a real threat to vegetation regrowth and could affect the future of some butterfly species, including the Black Hairstreak.

Adult

The male's forewings have an inconspicuous sex brand and less extensive orange markings on all wings. The ground colour of the wings of both sexes is similar, and is more golden orange than the White-letter Hairstreak, with a less distinct 'W'.

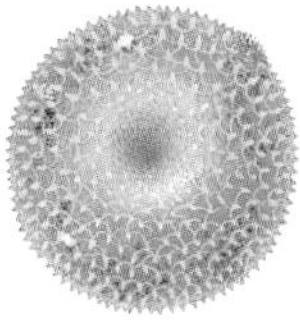

♂

♂

♀

♀

× 22

Egg

Well camouflaged and hard to find, the eggs are laid singly in the fork of a Blackthorn twig, where they remain for about nine months.

Chrysalis

Attached to a twig by a silken pad and girdle, the chrysalis resembles a bird dropping, but many still fall prey to insectivorous birds.

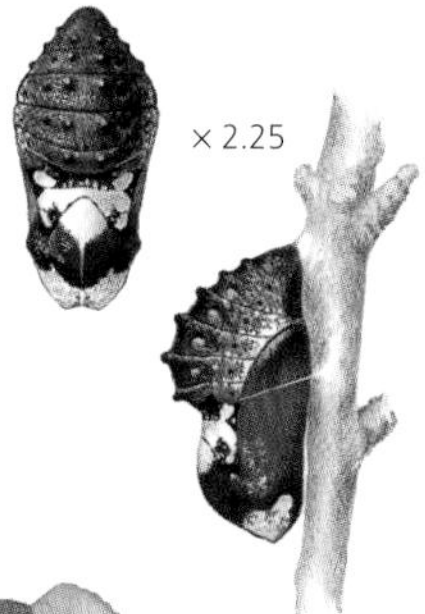

× 2.25

Caterpillar

Beautifully concealed, the caterpillar changes its appearance as the Blackthorn buds burst and expand. It feeds for two months before pupating.

× 2.25

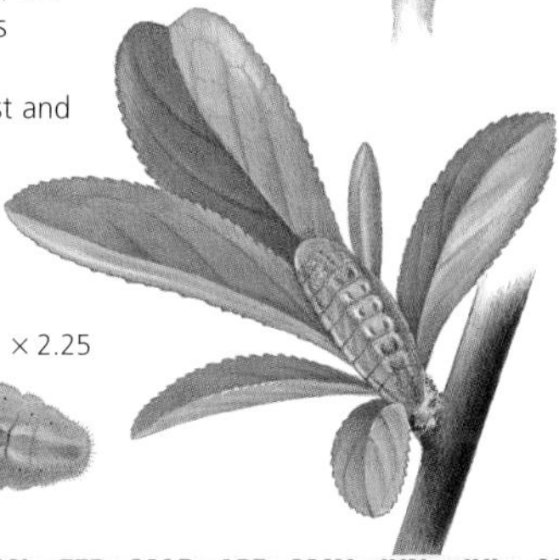

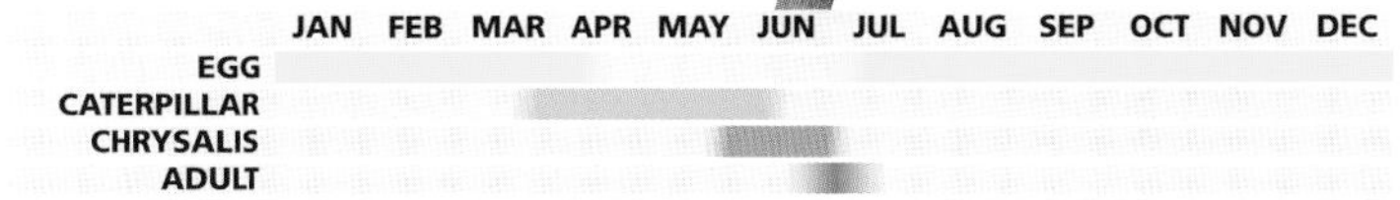

	JAN	FEB	MAR	APR	MAY	JUN	JUL	AUG	SEP	OCT	NOV	DEC
EGG												
CATERPILLAR												
CHRYSALIS												
ADULT												

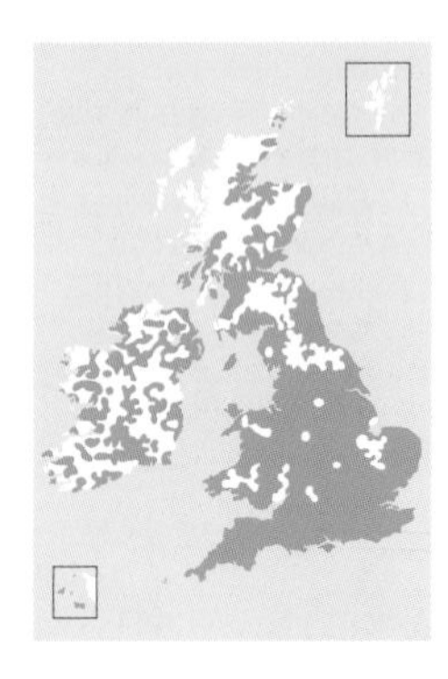

Small Copper

Lycaena phlaeas

Despite his size, the male Small Copper is a quarrelsome, restless little butterfly, ready to take on any intruder that ventures into his chosen sunny territory. He is fond of perching near or on the ground and can be seen in a wide range of habitats throughout Britain and Ireland. The Small Copper occurs in small, self-contained colonies on flowery hillsides, heaths and woodland rides, but it is a mobile species that will also colonise waste ground and roadside embankments and may sometimes visit gardens, although usually in small numbers.

This is a butterfly that thrives in hot, sunny conditions and in good years three or even four broods may be produced, lasting from late April until November. However, in cool wet summers populations crash and may take several years to recover. Overall, there has been a general decline in the fortunes of the Small Copper, particularly in north Wales. In East Anglia, agricultural intensification has made it hard for this and several other species to survive. It is, nevertheless, still a

Feeding
Common Fleabane is a popular nectar source for the Small Copper.

common and delightful little butterfly, whose brilliance would be greatly missed were it to disappear from our countryside.

The only other British butterfly with coppery wings is the Large Copper, which has recently died out from its one remaining site in Cambridgeshire (see page 136).

Adult
The male is usually smaller, with more pointed wings. Later broods are often larger and brighter. Specimens known as form *caeruleopunctata*, with a row of blue spots on the hindwings, are quite common, with occasional albinos also turning up.

Egg
Resembling a tiny golf ball, the eggs are laid singly, either near the midrib or undersurface of Common and Sheep's Sorrel, and occasionally dock leaves. The caterpillar emerges after a week.

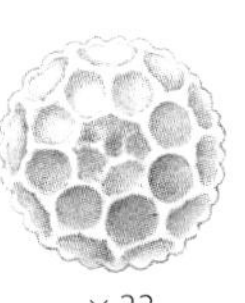
× 22

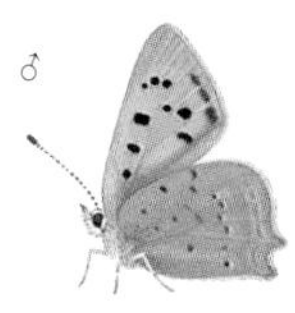
♂

albino form

♀

× 2.25

form *caeruleopunctata*

Caterpillar
The young, woodlouse-shaped caterpillar makes characteristic opaque grooves on the leaves as it feeds. When fully grown it can often be found at rest on the underside of the leaves. The caterpillar stage can last for about six months.

Chrysalis
The chrysalis is formed among leaves near the ground, where it remains for about a month.

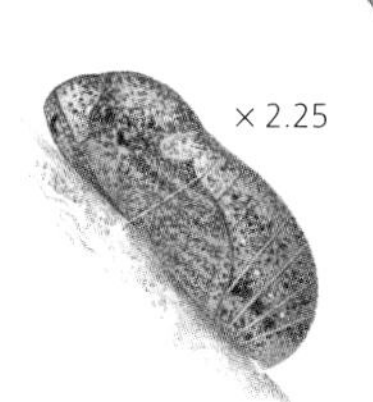
× 2.25

JAN FEB MAR APR MAY JUN JUL AUG SEP OCT NOV DEC
EGG
CATERPILLAR
CHRYSALIS
ADULT

Small Blue

Cupido minimus

The smallest and possibly the most inconspicuous British butterfly, the Small Blue is a delicate but drab little species, which is easily overlooked by those searching chalk downland for its more flamboyant relatives. In addition to calcareous grassland, it is also found in discrete self-contained colonies along roadsides, railway embankments and sheltered dunes where Kidney Vetch grows in abundance. Most of these colonies are fairly small, but some healthy colonies may contain many hundreds of butterflies. The flight period is from mid-May to late June, with an occasional second brood in late July and August.

Males spend much of their lives resting on vegetation, often close to one another, ready to mate with females or to challenge other males. They also congregate to feed from moist ground or from flowers such as Common Bird's-foot-trefoil and Horseshoe Vetch. After mating, the female can be seen flying around the flowerheads of Kidney Vetch, searching for suitable egg-laying sites.

Because of its small size, the Small Blue should be easy to recognise, although in

Feeding
Kidney Vetch, the caterpillar's foodplant, is also used by the adults as a nectar source.

flight it could be mistaken for the Brown Argus, which often flies in the same habitat. At rest, however, it is unmistakable, with its unmarked upperside and lightly spotted, pearl-grey underside, devoid of any orange.

The Small Blue is a butterfly in decline, and although colonies are widely distributed throughout Britain and Ireland, many are small and isolated.

Adult
The female's upperwings are plain brown, while the male has a silvery-blue dusting of scales near the base of the wings. The undersides of both sexes are similar, without orange, rather like a small Holly Blue but with a less silvery-blue ground colour.

♂

♀

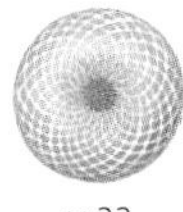

× 22

Egg
The tiny eggs are quite easy to find between the downy calyces of Kidney Vetch. They are laid singly but several may be found on the same flowerhead. They hatch after about a week.

× 2.25

Chrysalis
The chrysalis lasts for about two weeks, and is formed close to the ground in April or early May, often in association with ants.

probing the ground for salts

Caterpillar
The young caterpillar burrows into the calyx to feed on the developing seeds, although it will also eat other caterpillars it encounters. When fully grown, it lives exposed on the flowerheads, where it is easy to find. It then descends to the ground to spend the winter sheltered among mosses or in crevices.

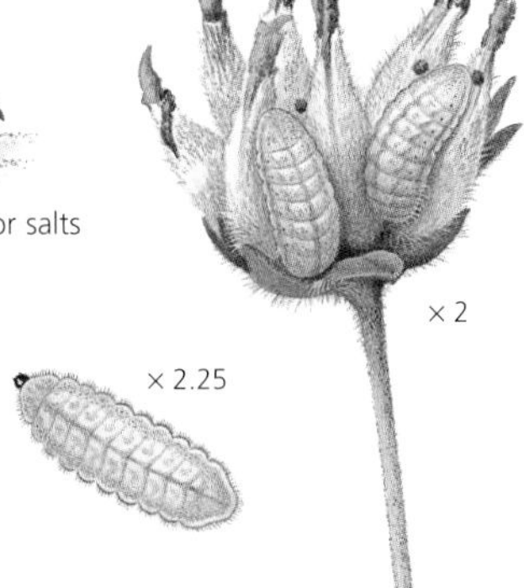

× 2

× 2.25

	JAN	FEB	MAR	APR	MAY	JUN	JUL	AUG	SEP	OCT	NOV	DEC
EGG												
CATERPILLAR												
CHRYSALIS												
ADULT												

Silver-studded Blue

Plebeius argus

This attractive little blue is most often associated with the heathlands of southern England, where it can occur in very large numbers. However, in many places it is in serious decline, mainly as a result of the destruction of heaths and the shading out of the sparsely vegetated, sunny habitats it prefers. The fragmentation of its habitat has led to populations becoming isolated and, further north, many have been lost altogether. The species also occurs on coastal dunes in Cornwall and occasionally on chalk and limestone grassland, with strong populations being found on Great Ormes Head, in north Wales, and the Isle of Portland, in Dorset.

Adults generally fly from late June until the end of August, in a single generation, although in north Wales they are on the wing two weeks earlier. This population is also unusual in that the butterflies are smaller and

Resting
Male and female resting on Gorse, one of several larval foodplants.

the females are bluer.

The male can be distinguished from the Common Blue by the thicker black margins to the wings, although the more variable female is best separated by looking at the underside. Here, the black marginal spots on the hindwings are studded with silvery-blue centres, hence the name, and the forewings lack the cell spot nearest the body. This spot is also absent in the similar Brown Argus, but that species has a different pattern of spots on the hindwings. The upperside of the Brown Argus also has brighter, more clearly defined orange spots, with no hint of blue.

Adult

Males are fairly constantly marked, with broad black wing margins on the upper surface, and are the smallest of the 'blue' blues. Females vary, from being dark brown with just a few blue scales on the wing surface close to the body, to being predominantly blue further north. The crescent-shaped markings are a duller orange than in the Brown Argus.

Egg

The large eggs are laid singly, close to the ground, on tender shoots of various heathers, gorses, Common Bird's-foot-trefoil, Common Rock-rose and Horseshoe Vetch. The fully formed caterpillar remains inside the egg until the following March.

× 22

♂

♀

× 2.25

Chrysalis

Formed underground in an ant nest, the chrysalis is cared for by ants, which also protect the vulnerable, freshly emerged adult butterfly.

female from north Wales

× 2.25

Caterpillar

The caterpillar stage lasts for about three months, during which time it is closely attended by black ants which feed on sugary secretions from glands on its body.

	JAN	FEB	MAR	APR	MAY	JUN	JUL	AUG	SEP	OCT	NOV	DEC
EGG												
CATERPILLAR												
CHRYSALIS												
ADULT												

Brown Argus

Aricia agestis

Until the 1990s, the Brown Argus had steadily declined as chalk and limestone grasslands were lost to agricultural improvement throughout southern and central England and Wales. Since then, however, it has made a comeback and has increased its range rapidly to the north and east, managing to adapt to other habitats such as railway cuttings, roadside verges and rough, overgrown land created by set-aside. In recent years, there has been a slight reversal in its expansion, possibly linked to cooler, wetter summers.

The Brown Argus is also found in a range of other habitats, such as heathland, dunes and woodland rides, where it usually lives in small colonies. However, numbers vary greatly from year to year, and some individuals wander and may be encountered unexpectedly. Adults appear in two broods a year, starting in May and lasting until the end of September. In north Wales, the Peak District and Yorkshire Wolds, it is usually single-brooded.

Females of several species of blue can be

♂

♀

Resting
Male and female Brown Argus on Common Rock-rose, the preferred foodplant on chalk downland.

confused with the Brown Argus, but it is smaller than most and its dark bronze-brown ground colour and clearly defined orange markings, without a trace of blue, make it a much smarter little butterfly. Worn specimens are best confirmed from the underside, where the lack of a spot in the cell of the forewing, near the body, and the almost vertical twin-spots on the top edge of the hindwing are conclusive. In flight the Brown Argus appears silvery grey, with a similarity to the Small Blue. By comparison, the female Common Blue is distinctly blue-grey.

♂ ♂ ♀ ♀

Adult
The female is larger, with more rounded wings and bolder orange markings that reach the wing tips. These markings taper off in the male and are sometimes absent. The fringes of the wings may have some dark chequering.

Egg
The eggs are laid singly on the underside of the leaves of Common Rock-rose on calcareous soils, while in other places various crane's-bills and Common Stork's-bill are used. The caterpillar hatches in a week.

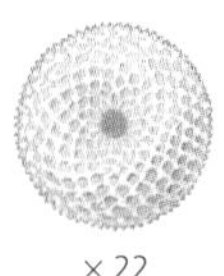

× 22

Chrysalis
The chrysalis is formed near the ground under the foodplant, surrounded by a few threads of silk and attended by ants. The adult emerges after two weeks.

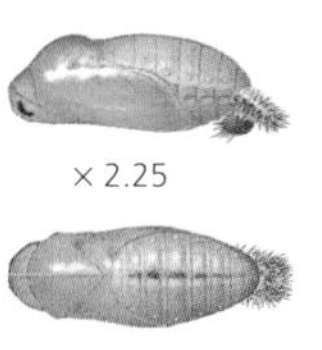

× 2.25

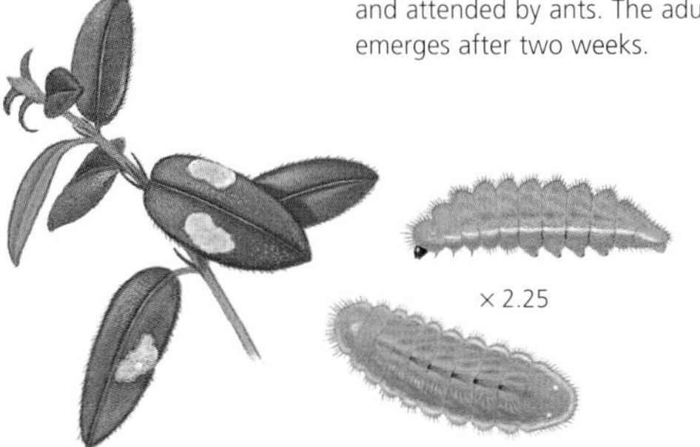

× 2.25

Caterpillar
Always accompanied by ants, the caterpillar rests and feeds on the underside of the leaves, creating transparent patches visible from above. Hibernation is spent in this stage.

	JAN	FEB	MAR	APR	MAY	JUN	JUL	AUG	SEP	OCT	NOV	DEC
EGG												
CATERPILLAR												
CHRYSALIS												
ADULT												

Northern Brown Argus

Aricia artaxerxes

This butterfly is the northern cousin of the Brown Argus. It occurs from Lancashire and south Cumbria northwards, and is found in small, sedentary colonies where its larval foodplant, Common Rock-rose, grows on sheltered, sunny hillsides. In the southern part of its range it has been declining gradually, but further north it is more secure, with probably many more colonies yet to be found.

In many ways it is similar in its behaviour and biology to the Brown Argus, but the main difference is that the Northern Brown Argus has only one brood a year. In northern England its flight period is from early June until mid-August, and in north-east Scotland from July until September. However, to confuse matters, Brown Argus colonies in north Wales, the Yorkshire Wolds and the Peak District, which were once regarded as a subspecies of the Northern Brown Argus, are also usually single-brooded. Scottish populations, subspecies *artaxerxes*, are distinctive: they are like the Brown Argus, but with

Resting
Male Northern Brown Argus on Common Rock-rose, the caterpillar's foodplant.

slightly reduced orange markings and a bright white spot in the centre of each forewing. The spots on the undersides are either pure white or minutely spotted with black. The northern England subspecies *salmacis* is much more like the Brown Argus. Here, the orange markings are reduced on the upperside, but the white spots are absent and on the underside the black spots are present, though not so prominent as in the Brown Argus.

Adult
The Northern Brown Argus is distinctive in Scotland. English populations are more weakly marked on both upper and undersides than the Brown Argus, and can be separated by their distribution.

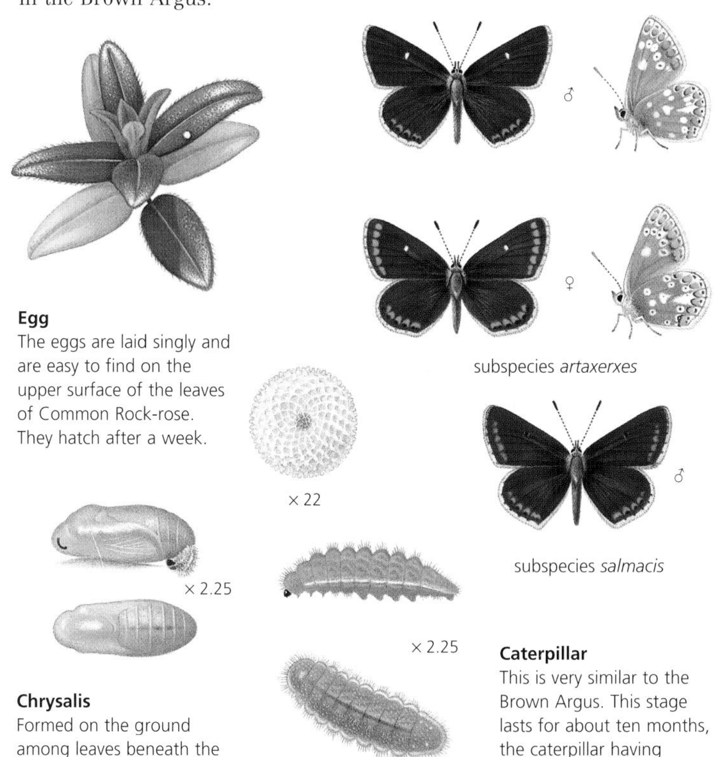

subspecies *artaxerxes*

subspecies *salmacis*

Egg
The eggs are laid singly and are easy to find on the upper surface of the leaves of Common Rock-rose. They hatch after a week.

Chrysalis
Formed on the ground among leaves beneath the foodplant and surrounded by a few strands of silk.

Caterpillar
This is very similar to the Brown Argus. This stage lasts for about ten months, the caterpillar having hibernated from October until the following spring.

	JAN	FEB	MAR	APR	MAY	JUN	JUL	AUG	SEP	OCT	NOV	DEC
EGG												
CATERPILLAR												
CHRYSALIS												
ADULT												

Common Blue

Polyommatus icarus

Fortunately, the Common Blue is still a regular sight in our countryside. It is the most widely distributed of the blues and is found from sea level to mountainsides throughout Britain and Ireland, except for Shetland. Occurring in a wide range of habitats – including damp, flowery meadows, heaths and woodland glades – it is also frequent in urban areas, along roadside verges, on uncultivated waste ground and in gardens.

It is generally double-brooded, flying in May and June, and again in August and September, but in the north of England, Scotland and Northern Ireland there is only one brood, which normally flies from June until September. In long, hot summers, however, an extra brood may appear, lasting into late October.

The male's violet-blue wings, finely edged with black and with clear, white wing margins, help separate the species from other blues. At rest, the underside of the

Feeding
A male Common Blue on Common Bird's-foot-trefoil, one of the caterpillar's foodplants.

hindwings lacks the twin vertical spots of the Brown Argus. These two species, along with other close relatives, may be found roosting communally, head downwards, among grasses and flowerheads.

Females also have white wing fringes, separating them from the rarer Adonis and Chalkhill Blues. Females are also variable, and range from the usual brown form, with a hint of blue, to beautiful blue varieties with orange margins. The most lovely of these, subspecies *mariscolore*, is found in Ireland and north-west Scotland.

Egg

Eggs are laid singly, on the tender leaves of a wide range of legumes, including Common Bird's-foot-trefoil, Black Medick, Common Restharrow, clovers and Greater Bird's-foot-trefoil. The caterpillar emerges after nine days.

Chrysalis

Pupation takes place on or near the ground beneath the foodplant, often by ant nests. The chrysalis stage lasts about two weeks.

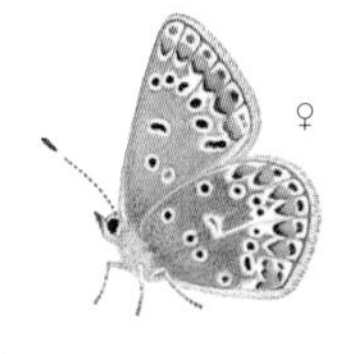

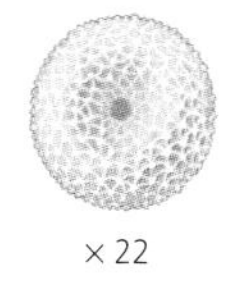

× 22

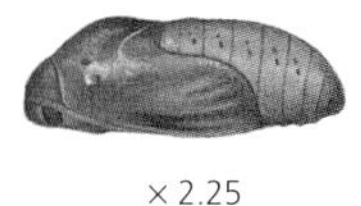

× 2.25

Caterpillar

The plain green caterpillar stage lasts for six weeks, although later in the year those that hibernate spend ten months in this stage.

× 2.25

Adult

The undersides of the sexes are similar, although the female is slightly browner. The underside of the Holly Blue, which may fly in the same habitat, is quite different, being pale blue with fine black spots.

	JAN	FEB	MAR	APR	MAY	JUN	JUL	AUG	SEP	OCT	NOV	DEC
EGG												
CATERPILLAR												
CHRYSALIS												
ADULT												

Chalkhill Blue

Lysandra coridon

This beautiful, silvery-blue butterfly, so characteristic of warm chalk and limestone hillsides, has declined throughout the last century, mainly as a result of the ploughing of its downland habitat. The cessation of grazing by sheep and also by rabbits, following myxomatosis, has hastened this decline, allowing the flowery sward to become overgrown and unsuitable.

Nevertheless, the species is still widespread and stable in much of southern England, and in some places populations may be huge. There can be no finer sight than dozens of male Chalkhill Blues feeding from the purple flowers of knapweeds and scabiouses on a hot summer's day, for it is a butterfly of high summer, appearing in a single brood between mid-July and September.

Feeding
Purple flowers such as knapweeds are a favourite nectar source.

When butterfly collecting was at its peak, aberrations of the Chalkhill Blue were the most highly prized targets, and hundreds of named varieties still exist in collections.

There is no mistaking the male, but the more secretive female can present problems. The larger size and chequered wing fringes tell the female apart from the Common Blue, and the underside appears darker, with less obvious orange crescents. The female Adonis Blue also has chequered wing fringes, but the pale scales around the outer edges of the spots on the upper hindwing are silvery white in the Chalkhill Blue, rather than blue. The Adonis Blue is also a slightly smaller and rather neater butterfly.

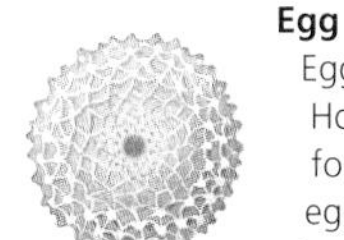

× 22

Egg

Eggs are laid singly on or around Horseshoe Vetch plants. The fully formed caterpillar remains inside the eggshell throughout the winter until the following spring.

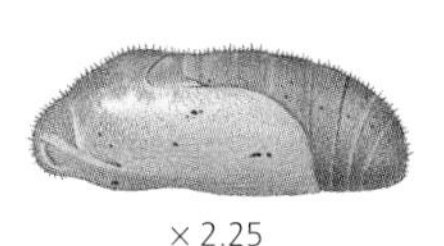

× 2.25

Chrysalis

The slightly hairy chrysalis is formed in a cell, on or under the ground, in the company of ants.

Caterpillar

The caterpillar is a lighter green than the Adonis Blue. Always accompanied by ants, it feeds at night and is fully grown in early June, after about ten weeks.

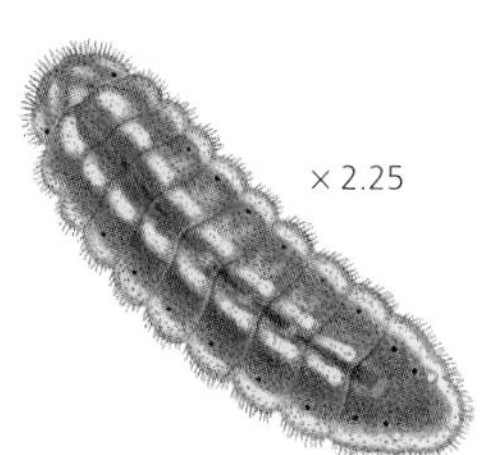

× 2.25

Adult

Females occasionally appear with the blue markings of the male, but most variation occurs in the spotting on the undersides.

	JAN	FEB	MAR	APR	MAY	JUN	JUL	AUG	SEP	OCT	NOV	DEC
EGG												
CATERPILLAR												
CHRYSALIS												
ADULT												

Adonis Blue

Lysandra bellargus

The Adonis Blue is the most brilliant, but sadly the rarest, of our downland blues. It is found only on the downs of southern England, at the northern edge of its European range, where it shares many of the habitat requirements of the Chalkhill Blue. The Adonis Blue is even more particular and needs short, herb-rich turf, on sunny south-facing slopes. In the last few hundred years it has suffered the same decline as its larger relative, as a result of agricultural intensification. However, in more recent decades, with the help of careful management, increased grazing and the recovery of rabbit populations, its numbers have risen.

It has two broods a year, the first appearing from mid-May until the end of June and the second from early August until the end of September, when populations are larger and it is sometimes seen in the company of the Chalkhill

♂

♀

Feeding
Horseshoe Vetch is used as a nectar source in early summer.

Blue. The Adonis Blue lives in sedentary colonies and rarely disperses far, making the colonies vulnerable to extinction if they are small and isolated from others.

The striking sky blue of the male is variable but distinctive, although when worn it could be mistaken for a Common Blue. However, the black lines cutting through the white fringes of the wings should separate the two species. The female Chalkhill Blue is a little larger, and has silvery-blue scales near the body and around the outer edge of the hindwing spots. The ground colour of the underside is also darker.

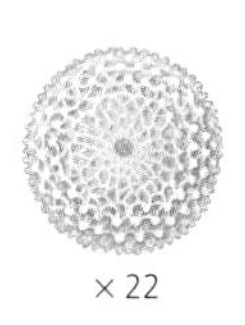

× 22

Egg
The eggs, laid on the underside of tender leaves of Horseshoe Vetch, are like those of the Chalkhill Blue but are more finely sculpted.

Chrysalis
Formed on or below the ground near ant nests, the shiny chrysalis lasts for about three weeks.

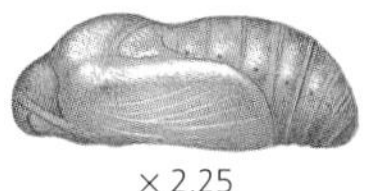

× 2.25

Adult
Some females may be predominantly blue. They are inconspicuous, spending much of their time feeding and crawling among Horseshoe Vetch, laying eggs.

× 2.25

Caterpillar
The caterpillar is best located by the obsessive attendance of red and black ants. It is a deeper green than the Chalkhill Blue, and is fully grown in late April or late July.

JAN FEB MAR APR MAY JUN JUL AUG SEP OCT NOV DEC

EGG

CATERPILLAR

CHRYSALIS

ADULT

Holly Blue

Celastrina argiolus

Unlike other blues, the Holly Blue is a butterfly of shrubby parks, woods, churchyards and gardens, where its nomadic lifestyle makes it a welcome sight from the end of March, with a second brood lasting until late September. Its habits more closely resemble those of the hairstreaks, as it often flies and basks high up on the foliage of trees and prefers to feed on aphid honeydew or salts from damp mud, rather than on flowers.

The range of the Holly Blue in Britain has expanded greatly in the last few decades, and it is now found as far north as Cumbria. In Ireland its distribution is more scattered. Populations vary greatly from year to year, due mainly to a combination of the climate and the presence of a parasitic wasp called *Listrodomus nycthemerus*. This black-and-yellow insect parasitises only the Holly Blue and kills large numbers of its caterpillars.

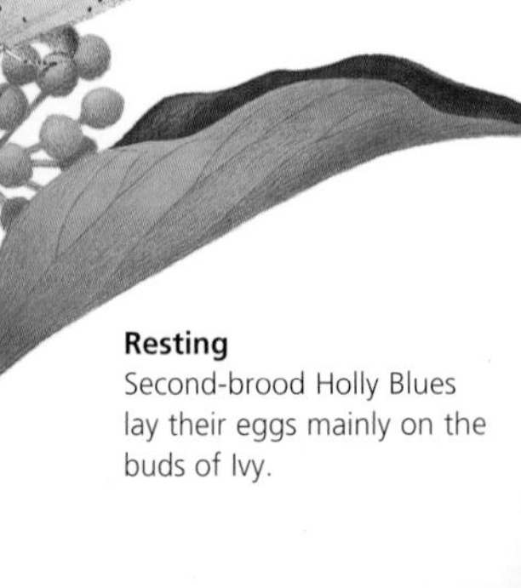

Resting
Second-brood Holly Blues lay their eggs mainly on the buds of Ivy.

The heavy black wing tips of the female make her easy to identify, but the lilac-blue male may be confused with the Common Blue, which sometimes flies in the same habitats. The black borders of the Holly Blue are bolder near the wing tips, and the white fringes are chequered with black. Also, both sexes have pale blue undersides.

Adult
The females of the second brood are a deeper purple and more heavily marked with black, but the males of both broods are identical. All undersides are alike.

Egg
The springtime females lay their eggs singly beneath the flower buds of Holly, but those of the summer brood lay mainly on Ivy, although Dogwood, Spindle, Snowberry, Pyracantha and a variety of other plants may be used. The eggs hatch after a week.

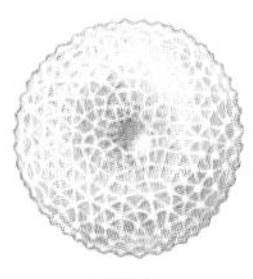
× 22

♀

first brood

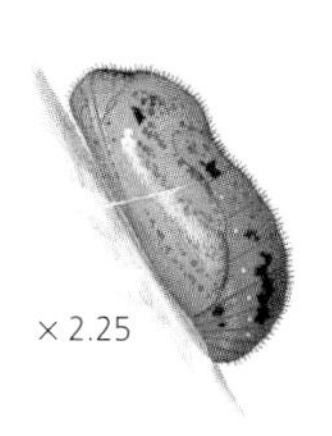
× 2.25

second brood

Chrysalis
The chrysalis from the first brood lasts for about 18 days, while the second brood chrysalis hibernates in this stage, attached in a crevice behind bark.

Caterpillar
Easy to find, especially on the developing buds of Ivy where feeding damage is obvious. It varies in colour and feeds for three to four weeks before pupation.

× 1.5

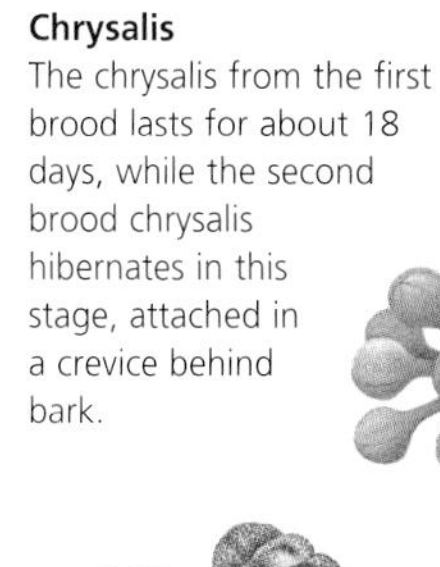
× 2.25

JAN FEB MAR APR MAY JUN JUL AUG SEP OCT NOV DEC

EGG
CATERPILLAR
CHRYSALIS
ADULT

Map showing the regions where the Large Blue has been reintroduced.

Large Blue

Maculinea arion

This impressive, light steely-blue butterfly was much prized by early butterfly collectors. It was lost from the British countryside, being finally declared extinct in 1979. The Large Blue was always a rare butterfly, with only about 90 known sites, and its decline was hastened by agricultural improvement, the abandonment of grazing and a lack of knowledge about the species' close relationship with the red ant *Myrmica sabuleti*. A few years after its extinction in Britain, when much more was known about its life history, the Large Blue was reintroduced using butterflies from Sweden, and it is now established on eight sites between the Cotswolds and south Devon.

It is a sedentary butterfly that requires herb-rich, acidic or limestone grassland which is well drained and grazed short, although formerly it was found on some sites on calcareous clay soil. It does well on coastal grasslands. Males patrol their breeding grounds searching for mates on warm sunny mornings, but in dull weather and

Feeding
Large Blues often use Wild Thyme as a nectar source.

in the heat of midday they rest among the vegetation. The female is less active, and after mating flutters around Wild Thyme plants searching for suitable egg-laying sites. The flight period is from mid-June until mid-July, in a single brood.

Despite the name 'Large Blue' some specimens may be quite small, but both wing surfaces of the male and female are distinctive and it is unlikely to be confused with any other species.

Adult
The female is usually larger, with heavier spotting, although this is very variable in both sexes.

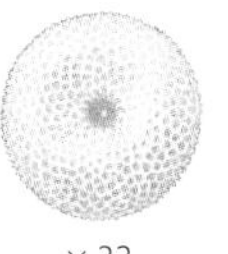

× 22

Egg
Eggs are laid singly, tucked into flowerheads of Wild Thyme growing among ant nests. The eggs hatch in about a week, depending on the temperature.

× 2.25

ant carrying caterpillar

caterpillar feeding on ant grubs

ant 'milking' caterpillar

Caterpillar
At first, the small caterpillar feeds on the flower seeds of Wild Thyme. After several weeks it drops to the ground and is soon found by ants, which feed on its sugary secretions. It begins to resemble an ant grub and is taken by an ant to the nest chamber. Here its diet changes and it becomes bloated, feeding on ant grubs until the following late May.

× 2.25

Chrysalis
The chrysalis is formed in the ant nest, where it remains for a further three weeks.

	JAN	FEB	MAR	APR	MAY	JUN	JUL	AUG	SEP	OCT	NOV	DEC
EGG												
CATERPILLAR												
CHRYSALIS												
ADULT												

Duke of Burgundy

Hamearis lucina

This rare and declining butterfly is the only member of the Metalmark (Riodininae) subfamily found in Britain or Europe. It most often occurs in small colonies on north- or west-facing slopes on scrubby chalk and limestone downland, but may also be found in coppiced areas and sunny woodland glades, where it used to be much more common.

Although from above it resembles some of the small fritillaries, its behaviour is distinctive. The male is the more conspicuous, perching on sunlit vegetation and darting out aggressively to confront intruders, but rarely straying far from his original perch. The female is much more secretive and spends much time resting, but wanders more widely than the male in search of foodplants for

Resting
Male and female Duke of Burgundy at rest on Cowslip.

egg-laying. Neither sex visits flowers very often. The single generation appears from early May until mid-June, although woodland colonies reach their peak a week or two later than those on downland sites.

The cessation of coppicing has reduced woodland populations dramatically, although on some downland sites the abandonment of spring and summer grazing has been beneficial. Light grazing in the autumn can help to prevent excessive scrub invasion, but large rabbit populations can be damaging as they reduce the sward height and prevent large Cowslip plants – the caterpillar's preferred foodplant – from flourishing. It is, therefore, only a delicate management-balancing act that will decide the future of this little butterfly.

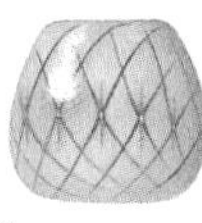

× 22

Egg
The eggs are laid singly or in small groups on the underside of the largest leaves of mainly Cowslips on downland and Primroses in woodland. They usually hatch after about two weeks.

Adult
The female is usually larger, with brighter, more rounded wings. Like other members of this subfamily of butterflies, the forelegs of the male are reduced and are not used for walking.

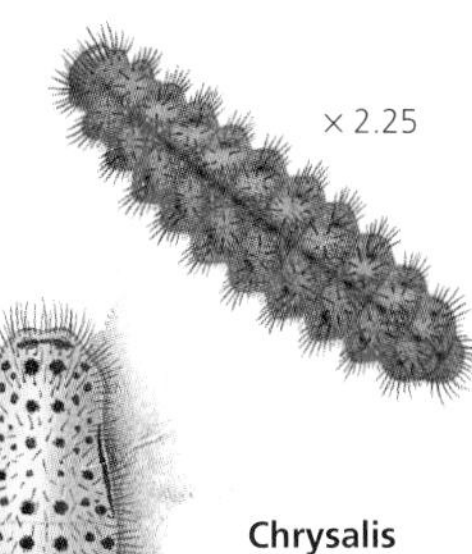

× 2.25

Caterpillar
The sluggish caterpillar rests by day at the base of the foodplant. It feeds at night causing distinctive damage to the leaves, leaving them perforated with small holes, with the veins and midrib intact. This stage lasts for about six weeks.

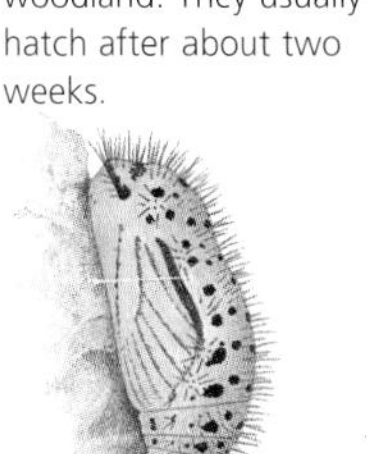

× 2.25

Chrysalis
The chrysalis is formed in the base of a grass tussock in July. It remains throughout the winter until the following May.

	JAN	FEB	MAR	APR	MAY	JUN	JUL	AUG	SEP	OCT	NOV	DEC
EGG												
CATERPILLAR												
CHRYSALIS												
ADULT												

White Admiral

Limenitis camilla

Found in most large deciduous woods in southern England, the White Admiral's fortunes have fluctuated in the past, but now it is more widespread than ever before, with recent expansions into eastern England and the West Midlands.

A graceful butterfly of sunlit woodland glades, the White Admiral has an elegance of flight equalled only by the Purple Emperor. Traditionally a butterfly of mature broadleaved woodlands, its range has been expanding and it may also be found in mixed conifer and deciduous plantations. It thrives in hot summers and can often be seen feeding on Bramble flowers, as well as salt from moist soil and dung. Its tolerance of shade has helped in its expansion, particularly since the cessation of coppicing and the tidying-up of woodlands.

The first adults appear in mid-June and the flight period lasts until the end of August, in a single brood. The Purple Emperor may sometimes be found in the same habitats as the

Basking
White Admiral basking on a Bramble leaf.

White Admiral and although both species feed on honeydew in the canopy, the White Admiral generally occurs lower down, when it can be separated by its smaller size and agile yet powerful gliding flight. Males are most often seen patrolling, and females, although more secretive, can be watched fluttering in the dappled light of woodland edges, searching for straggly growths of Honeysuckle on which to lay their eggs.

Adult

The sexes are similar but the female is usually slightly larger, with more rounded wings. There may be variation in the amount of white on the wings, with extreme examples, aberration *nigrina*, being all black.

♂

× 1.5

Egg

The attractive eggs, with their hairy honeycomb surface, are quite easy to find. They are laid singly, on the upper edge of a Honeysuckle leaf, where they remain for about a week before hatching.

× 15

Caterpillar

The young caterpillar feeds on either side of the midrib at the leaf tip. Here it rests, camouflaging itself by adorning the midrib and its body with its own droppings. It hibernates while still small in a leafy shelter called a hibernaculum, and resumes feeding in the spring. This stage lasts for ten months.

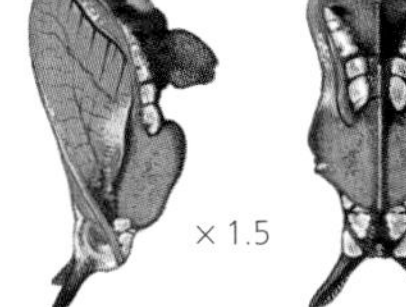

Chrysalis

Sprinkled with silvery spots that resemble dewdrops, this is perhaps the most attractive butterfly chrysalis. It remains in this stage, suspended below a stem, for about two weeks.

JAN FEB MAR APR MAY JUN JUL AUG SEP OCT NOV DEC

EGG
CATERPILLAR
CHRYSALIS
ADULT

Purple Emperor

Apatura iris

An elusive prize for butterfly enthusiasts, the handsome male Purple Emperor spends most of the day perching in the canopy of a particular favourite oak, or other 'master tree', rising occasionally to battle with other males, glinting high above the treetops. Sometimes, usually mid-morning, the male descends to feed from damp puddles, animal droppings or even decaying carcasses, providing photographers with their best opportunities. This is a butterfly of large mature broadleaved forests, where sunny rides support good growths of sallows, the caterpillar's foodplant.

The female lacks the rich, iridescent purple sheen of the male and is rarely seen. After mating in the treetops, she descends to search for suitable sallows for egg-laying. These are usually in partial shade and egg-laying normally occurs between two and four o'clock in the afternoon.

The flight period of the Purple Emperor is from late June until the end of August.

The Purple Emperor has been in steady decline for many decades, having disappeared from many woods in central England and Wales as a result of the destruction and fragmentation of its ancient woodland habitat. However, adults are capable of dispersing along hedgerows and across fields.

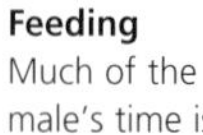

Feeding
Much of the male's time is spent feeding from leaves covered in aphid honeydew.

Chrysalis
The elegant green chrysalis hangs, perfectly camouflaged, beneath a sallow leaf for about two weeks.

Adult
The difference between the sexes is clear, although the undersides are similar. Variation is unusual but rarely the white is reduced, aberration *iolata*, or virtually absent, aberration *lugenda*.

Egg
The eggs are laid singly on the upper edge of a sallow leaf or, more rarely, on Grey Willow or Crack-willow, and hatch after about two weeks.

Caterpillar
The young caterpillar hibernates in a forked twig or near a leaf bud, which it closely resembles. It resumes feeding in the spring, when it turns green. The whole caterpillar stage lasts for about ten months.

Numbers vary from year to year, but this is usually a common butterfly that occurs in many habitats throughout Britain and Ireland, and is more frequent now than at any other time.

Red Admiral

Vanessa atalanta

The dramatic colours of the Red Admiral make it one of the most easily recognisable and familiar garden butterflies, yet this is an immigrant whose numbers depend on migration from North Africa and southern Europe. In recent years, however, there have been reports of Red Admirals in December and January, suggesting evidence of successful overwintering.

Having already mated, the major influx of migrants appears in late May and June. They gradually spread northwards, with reinforcements continuing until August, and the resulting adults lasting until November. From mid-August the Red Admirals begin to move south and a partial

Feeding
The Red Admiral often visits sedums in late summer and autumn.

re-migration takes place. On occasion, large numbers can be seen gathering along the south coast, preparing to head across the Channel.

Garden flowers, especially purple buddleias, sedums and Michaelmas-daisies, are often visited, and in the autumn the flowers of Ivy and rotting fruit are great favourites.

Adult

The sexes are alike. The upperside is unmistakable but when at rest, particularly when roosting with the forewings obscured, the pale blotch on the top edge of the hindwings is diagnostic.

Egg

The small eggs are laid singly on the upper surface of young nettle leaves, more rarely on Pellitory-of-the-wall. The eggs hatch after a week.

× 22

Caterpillar

The young caterpillar constructs a small tent at the base of a leaf. It remains hidden throughout its life and, as it grows, makes larger and more conspicuous tents. The caterpillar, which may be greyish yellow or predominantly black, feeds for about three weeks.

Chrysalis

The fully grown caterpillar constructs a final tent from several nettle leaves and pupates, suspended from the roof of the tent. These tents are easy to find from July until October.

× 1.5

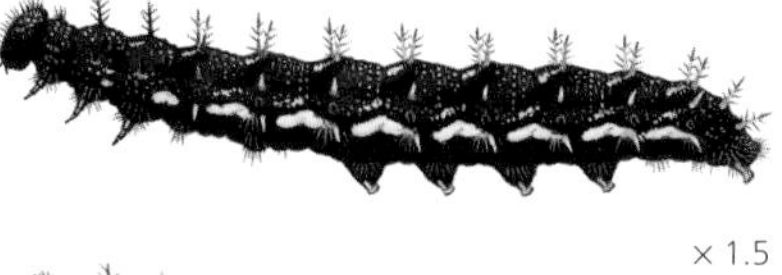

× 1.5

	JAN	FEB	MAR	APR	MAY	JUN	JUL	AUG	SEP	OCT	NOV	DEC
EGG												
CATERPILLAR												
CHRYSALIS												
ADULT												

Most years, migrants from North Africa and the Middle East reach Britain in May and June, mating and laying their eggs as they spread northwards, their numbers reinforced throughout the year by migrants from mainland Europe.

Painted Lady

Vanessa cardui

The Painted Lady is one of the best-known and most widely-distributed migratory butterflies in the world. It is a regular visitor to Britain and Ireland, but numbers vary greatly from year to year, with occasional mass migrations. The most recent of these, in 1996, was one of the largest ever recorded, when many millions arrived and could be seen almost everywhere, feasting on buddleias and other garden flowers throughout the country. In Britain, although it may have several broods, which can last into October or November, the Painted Lady appears unable to survive our cold, wet winters.

An unmistakable butterfly, the Painted Lady is found mainly in warm, open, flowery places. It has a strong, purposeful flight but spends much of its time basking on the

Resting
Painted Lady on mallow, an alternative foodplant.

ground, absorbing the sun's rays. As its main larval foodplants are various thistle species, it may even be found in intensively-farmed locations where few other butterflies are able to exist.

Adult
When freshly emerged, the Painted Lady has a beautiful rose-pink flush to its wings, fading in time to light orange. The sexes are similar. Some specimens may be very small.

× 22

Egg
The eggs are laid singly. Various species of thistle are preferred but mallows, nettles and Viper's-bugloss may also be used. They hatch after about a week.

Chrysalis
Variable in colour, the chrysalis is suspended within a tent of leaves for two weeks before hatching.

× 1.5

Caterpillar
The caterpillar spends most of its life in a tent of leaves. It is similar to the Red Admiral but is more slender, with a continuous yellow line along the sides. When fully grown, after about four weeks, it lives more openly on the leaves.

× 1.5

	JAN	FEB	MAR	APR	MAY	JUN	JUL	AUG	SEP	OCT	NOV	DEC
EGG												
CATERPILLAR												
CHRYSALIS												
ADULT												

Small Tortoiseshell

Aglais urticae

Two broods occur in the south, while in Scotland there is only one, with individuals often appearing darker as a result of the cooler conditions. Butterflies from the second brood show no interest in mating and in August they prepare for hibernation, often being found in houses, sheds and outbuildings, as well as in caves and hollow trees away from habitation.

Adults of this common resident butterfly can be found in almost any month of the year, but the Small Tortoiseshell is most familiar in gardens in late autumn, where it feeds from many cultivated flowers such as marigolds, buddleias and Michaelmas-daisies. It is widely distributed throughout Britain and Ireland and occurs in many habitats, including urban areas, intensively cultivated land and even mountain-tops.

This is one of the first butterflies to appear after hibernation, usually on warm, sunny days in March, when sallow catkins or dandelions are visited. The male is strongly territorial, and after feeding in the morning spends the rest of the day

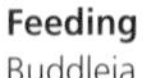

Feeding
Buddleia is a great favourite of the Small Tortoiseshell.

inspecting any dark objects that approach his transitory territory, spiralling high into the sky with rival males or tenaciously pursuing females. Following pairing, which may last throughout the night, the female spends the afternoons egg-laying, choosing young growths of nettles in sunny sheltered places.

Adult

The sexes are alike, but some individuals exposed to high temperatures in the chrysalis stage occasionally appear with reduced orange and the dark spots fused together, aberration *semi-ichnusoides*.

aberration *semi-ichnusoides*

Chrysalis

The chrysalis may be golden or more cryptically coloured. It is suspended, sheltered beneath a ledge or wall, or sometimes from a dried stem of the foodplant. The adult emerges after 12 days.

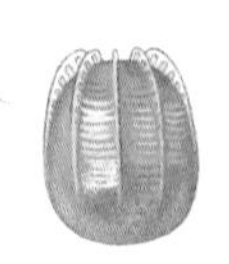

× 15

Egg

Large clusters, sometimes containing several hundred eggs, are laid on the underside of young Common and Small Nettle leaves, growing in sunlight.

× 1.5

Caterpillar

The young caterpillars are gregarious at first, living in a conspicuous untidy web until almost fully grown. They then disperse and live separately, exposed on the nettle leaves. They range in colour from variegated yellow to nearly all black, and spend about four weeks as a caterpillar.

× 1.5

	JAN	FEB	MAR	APR	MAY	JUN	JUL	AUG	SEP	OCT	NOV	DEC
EGG												
CATERPILLAR												
CHRYSALIS												
ADULT												

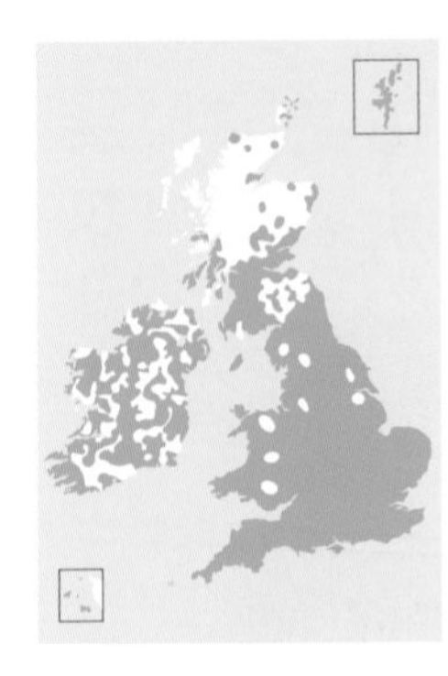

Apart from occasional cool wet summers, when numbers may be low, the Peacock seems to be gradually expanding its range northwards throughout England and Northern Ireland, although it is still rare in Scotland north of Argyll.

Peacock

Inachis io

The startling beauty of a freshly emerged Peacock, feasting with other insects on richly-scented sprays of Buddleia, is thankfully still a common sight on warm summer days, as this butterfly is a regular garden visitor which enjoys feeding from many nectar-rich cultivated flowers. It is also frequent in woodland glades, meadows and downland, where it feeds avidly from flowers such as knapweeds, teasels and thistles.

The Peacock is one of our most easily recognised butterflies when it is active, but may be confused with near relatives when it is at rest or hibernating. When alarmed, the Peacock flashes its staring eye-spots and produces a hissing sound by rubbing its wings together.

Peacocks are often the first butterflies to

Resting
Peacock at rest on Common Nettle, the main larval foodplant.

be seen in February or March, when they bask in the early spring sunshine, having hibernated from the previous September in hollow trees, sheds and woodpiles. The offspring of these hibernators emerge in July, when the Peacock is at its most abundant.

Adult

Both sexes are similar, although females are a little larger. Very rarely, specimens occur with 'blind' eye-spots on the hindwings. Peacocks can live for about ten months.

Chrysalis

This is suspended from a silken pad for about two weeks. The colour of the chrysalis varies according to its surroundings.

× 1.5

Egg

Dense clusters of up to 500 eggs (above) are laid on the underside of Common Nettle leaves. This may take up to two hours. Large, sheltered plants in sunny positions, often in the middle of nettle patches, are favoured. The eggs hatch after two weeks.

× 15

Caterpillar

Young caterpillars feed gregariously in untidy clusters, living among webs spun over the nettle tops. When fully grown they disperse to prepare for pupation. They are bigger than Small Tortoiseshell caterpillars, velvety black with rusty prolegs, and are covered in spines and minute white dots.

× 1.5

	JAN	FEB	MAR	APR	MAY	JUN	JUL	AUG	SEP	OCT	NOV	DEC
EGG												
CATERPILLAR												
CHRYSALIS												
ADULT												

Comma

Polygonia c-album

In the last 200 years the fortunes of the Comma have changed dramatically. Once common, it declined rapidly and by the 1920s it was almost extinct, apart from on the Welsh borders. Since then, and particularly in the last 20 years, its range has increased hugely.

The unique ragged outline of the Comma distinguishes it from all other butterflies, but on the wing it could be mistaken for a fritillary as its flight is rapid and interspersed with twisting glides. It is mainly found in open woodland rides and margins but it also occurs in orchards and gardens. It usually first appears in March and April, having hibernated, perfectly camouflaged on a branch or among leaves at the base of a tree trunk.

After setting up its territory, the male inspects all intruders in search of a female, sparring with rival males. Several factors, including temperature and day length, influence the development of caterpillars produced by springtime matings. In warm, early summers, when caterpillars are exposed to long periods of sunlight, larger proportions of the paler orange form *hutchinsoni* are produced in early July. These then mate and produce a second brood in August or September.

Feeding
In the autumn, Commas often feed from overripe fruit.

form *hutchinsoni*

Adult
The characteristic outline is less ragged in the female and the beautifully marbled underside is plainer. Both sides of form *hutchinsoni* are lighter than the typical form. Occasionally, aberrations occur with darkened suffused wings.

Chrysalis
The cryptically marked chrysalis is concealed among withered leaves for two weeks until the adult emerges.

Caterpillar
The young caterpillar lives on the underside of a leaf. When fully grown it rests exposed on the upperside, gaining protection from its resemblance to a bird dropping. This stage lasts for about seven weeks.

Egg
The eggs are laid singly on the upper edge of Hop or Common Nettle leaves, less often on currant and elm suckers. They hatch after two to three weeks.

JAN FEB MAR APR MAY JUN JUL AUG SEP OCT NOV DEC

EGG
CATERPILLAR
CHRYSALIS
ADULT

Small Pearl-bordered Fritillary

Boloria selene

Like most of our fritillaries, the Small Pearl-bordered Fritillary has disappeared from much of central, southern and eastern England as a result of the loss of woodlands and changes in their management. The butterfly survives best on the open moorland and damp grasslands of Scotland and Wales, and on coastal cliffs, dunes and scrubby slopes mixed with Bracken in the north-west and south-west of England.

The male has a rapid, gliding flight, and patrols low over vegetation searching for females. After mating, the female begins egg-laying around midday, flying close to the ground in search of violets.

The main flight period is from mid-May until mid-July in the south-west, where in warm summers a partial second

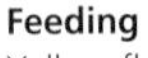

Feeding
Yellow flowers such as Creeping Buttercup are often used as a nectar source.

brood may appear in August. In Scotland, emergence may be a month later.

It sometimes flies in the same habitats as the Pearl-bordered Fritillary, with which it is easily confused, but the Pearl-bordered flies slightly earlier in the year and often looks worn by the time the Small Pearl-bordered Fritillary appears. Separation is best made from the underside, which in the Small Pearl-bordered Fritillary is brighter, with more silvery spots. There is also greater contrast and the veins are black. Its upperside is a brighter orange and the post-discal spot in space 4 (see lines in illustrations) is always closer to the margin.

♂

♂

Adult

The female is usually larger and in Scotland may be brighter, with paler yellow near the edge of the wings. There is sometimes variation in the size of spots and the suffusion around the base of the wings.

♀

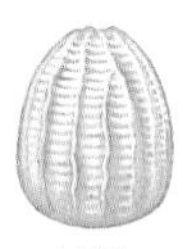

× 22

Egg

The eggs are laid singly, on or near Common Dog-violet or Marsh Violet. They hatch in ten to 12 days.

Chrysalis

This is suspended close to the ground near the foodplant, where it remains for two weeks.

× 1.5

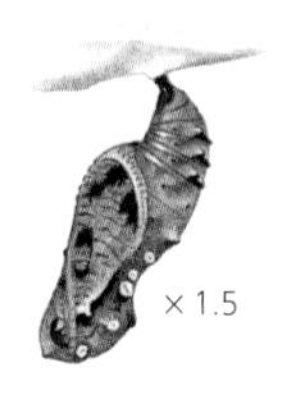

× 1.5

Caterpillar

Easily identified by the two forward-projecting spines, the caterpillar hibernates among dried leaves when half-grown. It resumes feeding in the spring, but is secretive and rarely seen. This stage lasts for ten to 11 months.

	JAN	FEB	MAR	APR	MAY	JUN	JUL	AUG	SEP	OCT	NOV	DEC
EGG												
CATERPILLAR												
CHRYSALIS												
ADULT												

Pearl-bordered Fritillary

Boloria euphrosyne

Once regarded as a common woodland butterfly, the Pearl-bordered Fritillary has declined even more rapidly than the Small Pearl-bordered Fritillary, with which it shares many characteristics. In England, it is a butterfly of woodland clearings and as such benefited early last century from widespread coppicing, but as this practice has declined, so have the fortunes of the Pearl-bordered Fritillary. In Scotland and Wales it is found in open deciduous woods, along woodland edges, in areas of grassland mixed with Bracken, and on scrub. The only place it is found in Ireland is on the limestone scrub of the Burren.

It is the earliest fritillary to appear, usually from mid-April until July in a single brood, though occasionally with a partial second brood in August. The male spends most

Feeding
Spring flowers such as Bugle are often visited for nectar.

sunny days patrolling, flapping and gliding in search of females and visiting the spring flowers of Bugle, Primrose and buttercups.

The Pearl-bordered Fritillary's similarity to the Small Pearl-bordered Fritillary can be confusing, but see that species (page 91) for key differences.

Adult

The female is usually larger, with a slightly paler ground colour, especially near the outer margins. Variation in the amount of black markings sometimes occurs.

♀

Egg

The eggs are laid singly, on or near various species of violet growing in sunny sheltered places. They hatch after two weeks.

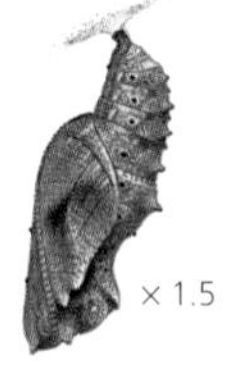

Chrysalis

The chrysalis is formed among withered vegetation close to the ground, and lasts for about three weeks.

Caterpillar

The caterpillar feeds from June until it is ready for hibernation, around September. It emerges in spring and spends the next month feeding, interspersed with bouts of basking in the sunshine. This stage lasts for about 11 months.

	JAN	FEB	MAR	APR	MAY	JUN	JUL	AUG	SEP	OCT	NOV	DEC
EGG												
CATERPILLAR												
CHRYSALIS												
ADULT												

In the last few decades, new research has helped the High Brown Fritillary and several well-managed colonies, particularly those on nature reserves in Cumbria, are doing well.

High Brown Fritillary

Argynnis adippe

None of our British butterflies has declined more rapidly than the High Brown Fritillary, which once occurred in most large woods in England and Wales as far as north as Cumbria. It is now found mainly in the Lake District and Dartmoor, with a few sites in between, totalling about 50 colonies. In these sites it occurs on rocky limestone outcrops scattered with trees, or on scrubby grassland, both habitats being dominated by Bracken.

Adults are fond of feeding from the flowers of Bramble and thistles and are easily approached, but in flight they are swift and elusive, and will disappear high into the foliage of trees if alarmed or if the weather is bad. Although the High Brown Fritillary lives in colonies, individuals frequently wander for several kilometres. Its single brood flies from mid-June until late August.

Hard to separate from the Dark Green Fritillary in flight, the underside of the hindwings is the best way to tell the two apart at rest. The High Brown Fritillary has a characteristic row of rust-red spots with silver centres.

Feeding
The High Brown Fritillary regularly visits Bramble flowers.

Adult
The outer margins of the forewings are usually straight or slightly concave. The male has thickened sex brands on veins two and three of the forewings. The female is usually larger than the male and often has bolder black spots. Variations on both surfaces occur; occasionally the silver spots on the underside are missing, aberration *cleodoxa*, more frequent in southern Europe.

Chrysalis
The chrysalis is suspended in a loose tent of leaves for three to four weeks.

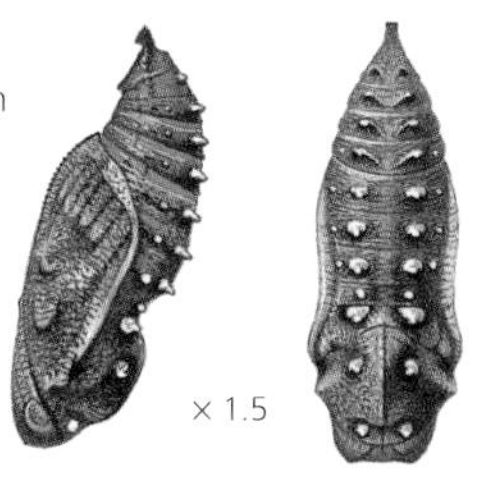

Caterpillar
The caterpillar stage lasts for about nine weeks. Beautifully camouflaged when resting on dried Bracken, it may be quite dark brown but the lighter greenish-brown form is more usual.

× 15

Egg
Laid singly among leaf litter near violets; the young caterpillar develops but remains in the egg until the following spring.

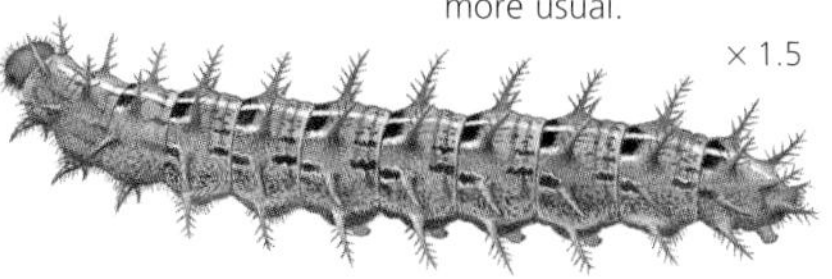

JAN FEB MAR APR MAY JUN JUL AUG SEP OCT NOV DEC
EGG
CATERPILLAR
CHRYSALIS
ADULT

Dark Green Fritillary

Argynnis aglaja

The fast, powerfully-flying Dark Green Fritillary is the most widespread of the large fritillaries. Found on open flowery downland, dunes, coastal cliffs, moorland and, less often, along sunny woodland rides, it often flies in damp places less favoured by other large fritillaries. It occurs throughout Britain and Ireland, although it has declined in particular in central and eastern England, largely as a result of the destruction and improvement of herb-rich grasslands.

The Dark Green Fritillary first appears in early June and flies in a single brood until early September. On hot days the male flies determinedly, often battling up windy hillsides in search of a mate, occasionally wandering far from his breeding ground. The female is more sedentary and

Feeding
Male Dark Green Fritillary feeding on Wild Privet.

after mating sets about her search for large clumps of violets growing in sunny, sheltered places. Both sexes are keen on purple downland flowers, such as thistles and knapweeds, but on dunes Wild Privet is a favourite.

Adult

The larger female is more ochreous, often with paler marginal spots. Scottish populations are often much more boldly and beautifully marked. The male has slightly thickened veins on the forewings, which are more rounded than those of the High Brown Fritillary.

♂

Egg

Laid singly close to lush growths of violets, the eggs hatch after two to three weeks.

× 15

Chrysalis

The distinctive curved chrysalis is suspended within a tent of grass stems held loosely with silk. Here it remains for about a month.

♀

× 1.5

Caterpillar

After hibernating when small, the caterpillar feeds actively in the daytime and pupates when it is nine months old.

× 1.5

JAN FEB MAR APR MAY JUN JUL AUG SEP OCT NOV DEC

EGG

CATERPILLAR

CHRYSALIS

ADULT

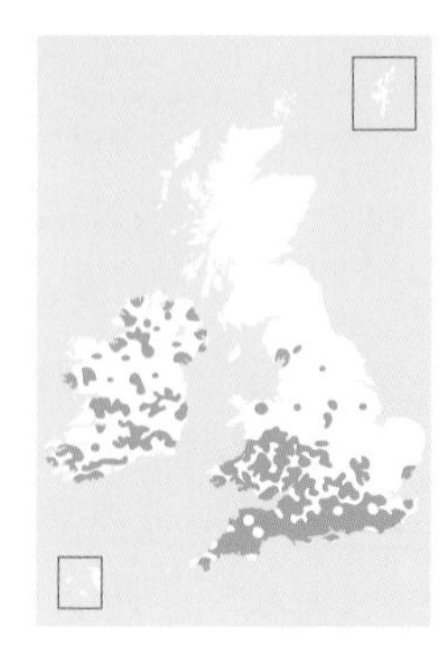

Silver-washed Fritillary

Argynnis paphia

This spectacular fritillary is still quite common in most large broadleaved woodlands in southern England. However, in Wales, Ireland and south-west England it also occurs along mixed hedgerows and lanes, and on uncultivated land bordering woods. Throughout the last century its populations have fluctuated, giving an overall decline, particularly from the north and east, but in recent decades there has been some re-expansion. Much of the general decline is linked with changes in woodland management, but climate change also affects populations.

A single brood flies from mid-June until early September, with peak numbers at the end of July, when on good sites many adults can be found jostling to feed on Bramble flowers in sunny glades. Males are the more conspicuous sex and patrol over large areas, swooping down from the treetops, gliding and twisting in the sunlight, in pursuit of females whom they court in a spectacular looping chase. Females can be seen fluttering in shadier parts of the wood, searching for clumps of violets growing at the base of oak trees.

Feeding
A female on Bramble flowers, the favourite nectar supply.

Adult
The male has four bold sex brands along the veins of the forewings. The markings on the undersides of both sexes are similar.

♂

Form *valezina*
In central and southern England, up to 15% of the females occur in the beautiful form called *valezina*, which is olive-green with an underside washed with pink.

♀

Chrysalis
Resembling a withered leaf, the chrysalis is suspended among vegetation from a silken pad for two to three weeks.

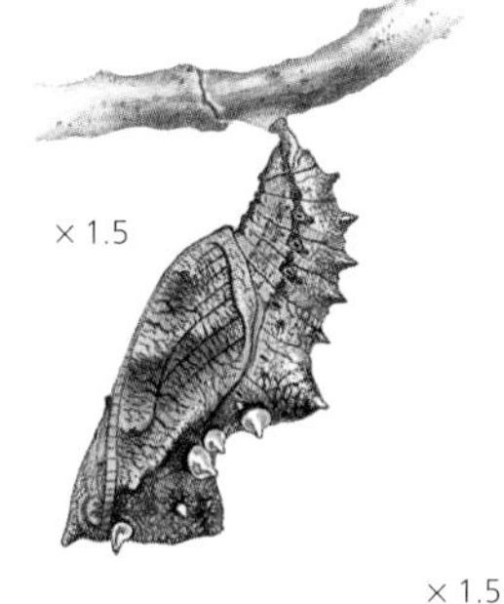

× 1.5

× 15

Egg
The eggs are laid singly, usually one to two metres up, in a crevice on the trunk of an oak, with Common Dog-violets growing nearby. They hatch after two weeks.

Caterpillar
After eating its eggshell, the young caterpillar hibernates in a crevice until spring when it descends to feed on leaves of Common Dog-violet. Its life is spent feeding and basking in the sun until it is fully grown, at ten months old.

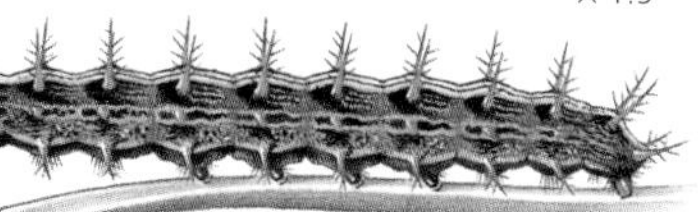

× 1.5

	JAN	FEB	MAR	APR	MAY	JUN	JUL	AUG	SEP	OCT	NOV	DEC
EGG												
CATERPILLAR												
CHRYSALIS												
ADULT												

Marsh Fritillary

Euphydryas aurinia

Although, as its name suggests, the Marsh Fritillary is found mainly in damp, flowery meadows and marshy woodland clearings, some colonies, especially in southern England, exist on drier downland slopes where lush growths of Devil's-bit Scabious or Small Scabious are found. This is a butterfly that is in serious decline throughout Europe, and in Britain it has been lost from most central and eastern counties. Drainage and overgrazing of damp grasslands have hastened this decline, resulting in the fragmentation of suitable habitats and preventing recolonisation from adjacent colonies. Small *Apanteles* wasps sometimes parasitise the caterpillars and can also hugely affect populations, which may be enormous one year and almost absent the next.

Marsh Fritillaries live in discrete colonies, males appearing a few

Feeding
Marsh Fritillaries often favour Meadow Thistle as a nectar source.

days before females, in a single brood from mid-May through until mid-July. Unlike other fritillaries, they are not powerful fliers, and not until the female has off-loaded her egg batch does she move further afield to feed and occasionally lay another smaller batch of eggs. Towards the end of the flight period, individuals of either sex may wander further from their breeding grounds.

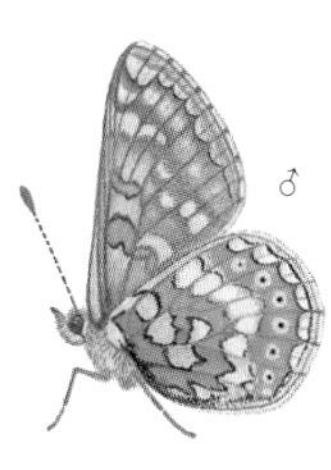

Egg
Laid in a batch of several hundred on the underside of a large leaf of Devil's-bit Scabious, growing in a warm sheltered position, the eggs darken gradually and hatch in about three weeks.

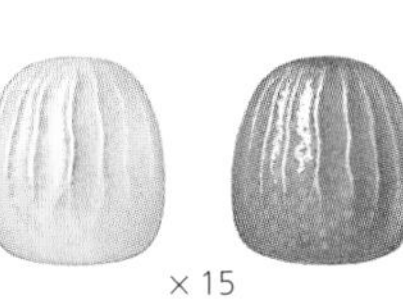

× 15

form *hibernica*

Chrysalis
The chrysalis is suspended for two weeks among vegetation near to the ground.

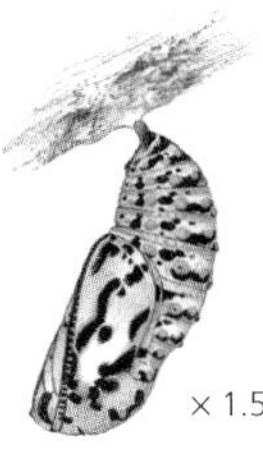
× 1.5

Adult
The female is usually larger, although small specimens of both sexes may occur. Aged, worn individuals take on a greasy appearance, hence the old name 'Greasy Fritillary'. In Ireland, the lovely bright form *hibernica* occurs.

Caterpillar
When young, the caterpillars live gregariously and hibernate in a thick silken retreat. They emerge in the spring and live conspicuously, feeding and basking together until fully grown. They then live solitarily before pupation, having spent ten months in this stage.

× 1.5

	JAN	FEB	MAR	APR	MAY	JUN	JUL	AUG	SEP	OCT	NOV	DEC
EGG												
CATERPILLAR												
CHRYSALIS												
ADULT												

Glanville Fritillary

Melitaea cinxia

Named after its discoverer of some 300 years ago, Lady Eleanor Glanville, this, our rarest fritillary, is almost confined to the crumbling undercliffs, chines and chalk downs in the southern half of the Isle of Wight and in the Channel Islands. Long ago, it was found in isolated places on the mainland, but apart from an introduced colony in Somerset, one small colony only has persisted in recent years on the Hampshire coast, near Christchurch. In Britain, it is at the extreme north-western edge of its distribution, and nearby, in mainland Europe it is found commonly in a variety of flowery habitats.

The Glanville Fritillary flies in a single brood from mid-May until the end of June, and rarely again in August in a partial second brood. An elegant, sun-loving butterfly, the territorial male is constantly on the wing, always on the

Resting
A female Glanville Fritillary resting on Ribwort Plantain.

lookout for females. Both sexes visit a variety of flowers such as Common Bird's-foot-trefoil and Thrift. Individuals are sometimes found away from known breeding sites, on occasion forming new colonies in suitable habitats, for this is a butterfly adapted to shifting, eroding soils where new growths of Ribwort Plantain flourish. Its present status and its future therefore depend on the continuance of this natural process.

As a result of its restricted distribution, the Glanville Fritillary is unlikely to be confused with any other butterfly, but the Marsh Fritillary does have a similar row of black spots on the hindwings, although its upperside is more variegated and the underside plainer.

Egg
Batches of 50 to 200 eggs are laid on the underside of leaves of Ribwort Plantain growing in warm, sheltered places. They hatch after about three weeks.

× 22

Caterpillar
The small caterpillars live communally in webs spun over plantains. They hibernate in the autumn and resume feeding conspicuously in the spring, basking on their webs in the sunshine. When fully grown at ten months old they disperse to prepare for pupation.

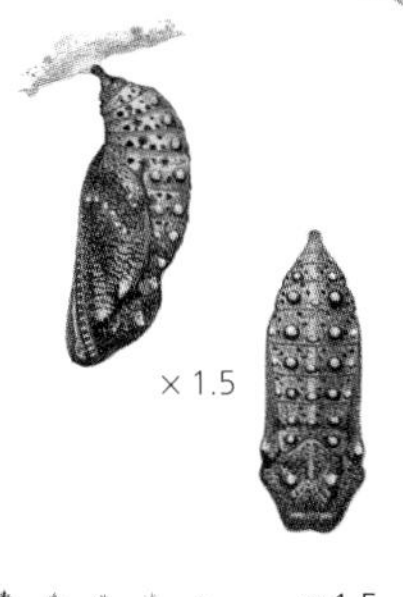
× 1.5

× 1.5

Adult
The female is larger than the male, and has more rounded and sometimes slightly ochreous wings.

Chrysalis
Formed in thick vegetation, the chrysalis stage lasts for about three weeks.

	JAN	FEB	MAR	APR	MAY	JUN	JUL	AUG	SEP	OCT	NOV	DEC
EGG												
CATERPILLAR												
CHRYSALIS												
ADULT												

Heath Fritillary

Melitaea athalia

Only about 40 colonies of this rare butterfly are left in Britain, but conservation efforts in Kent and Essex in the last 20 years have increased some populations, and in the south-west of England several new colonies have been discovered. It was traditionally a butterfly of acid woodlands in the south-east, where it roamed in search of newly coppiced areas with an abundance of its foodplant, Common Cow-wheat. However, the decline in the practice of cyclical coppicing was disastrous for the butterfly as many Heath Fritillary sites became overgrown and unsuitable.

Fortunately, colonies also exist in sheltered heathland valleys on Exmoor and on uncultivated flowery grassland in Devon and Cornwall. The Exmoor sites are owned by The National Trust and are well managed, but the grassland sites are isolated and more vulnerable.

This is a sedentary butterfly that only flies on warm sunny days. Males may sometimes be seen in huge numbers when the conditions are right, and both sexes visit a variety of nectar-rich flowers.

Adults appear from late May until early July in Cornwall, and in Exmoor and the

Resting
The Heath Fritillary is fond of basking on vegetation in the sunshine.

♂

south-east from mid June to early August. In the south-east there may be a small second brood in late August.

The Heath Fritillary's banded, chequered wings, which lack any spots, separate it from the two species of pearl-bordered fritillary, both of which also have diagnostic silvery 'pearls' on their undersides. The Marsh Fritillary's wings are more variegated and the hindwings have a distinctive row of black spots.

Adult
The intensity of the black markings varies, but generally the female is larger and more brightly marked than the male.

× 22

Egg
Laid in batches of up to 150, the eggs are positioned on the underside of leaves close to, but not actually on, foodplants such as Common Cow-wheat, Ribwort Plantain and Germander Speedwell. On Exmoor, Foxglove may sometimes be used. The eggs hatch after two to three weeks.

× 1.5

Chrysalis
The chrysalis is suspended, hidden among vegetation, for about two weeks.

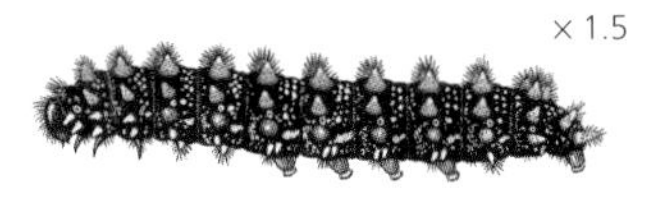
× 1.5

Caterpillar
Young caterpillars hibernate either in groups in a silken web or alone among dead leaves. They emerge in the spring, and feed conspicuously and bask in the sun until they are 11 months old.

	JAN	FEB	MAR	APR	MAY	JUN	JUL	AUG	SEP	OCT	NOV	DEC
EGG												
CATERPILLAR												
CHRYSALIS												
ADULT												

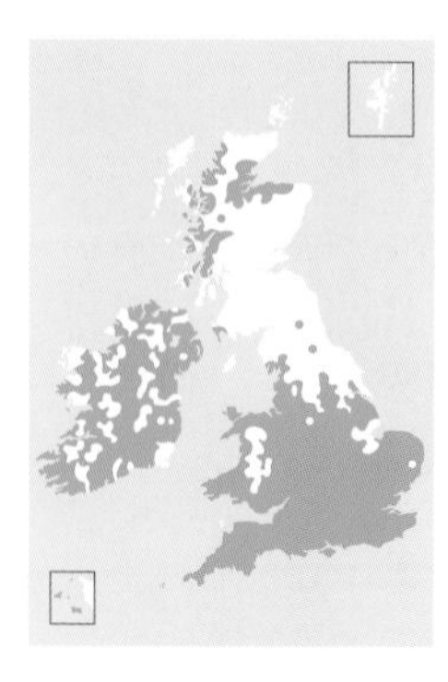

Since the 1930s the Speckled Wood, which had been in decline for 60 years, has expanded its range enormously and is now a common butterfly throughout the Midlands southwards, as well as in Wales, Ireland and parts of Scotland.

Speckled Wood

Pararge aegeria

The Speckled Wood is a butterfly of dappled woodland glades, with a greater tolerance of shade than most butterflies, and this appears to have benefited it following the cessation of coppicing. Long-term changes in the climate may also affect its future success, as populations increase and expand following cool, wet years and decrease when it has been dry.

The Speckled Wood may also be found along lanes and wooded hedgerows, and often visits gardens, where the territorial male perches on sunlit vegetation, spiralling into the air with rival males. It has been found that these more sedentary males tend to have four hindwing spots, whereas males that patrol in pursuit of females usually have three spots. Both sexes

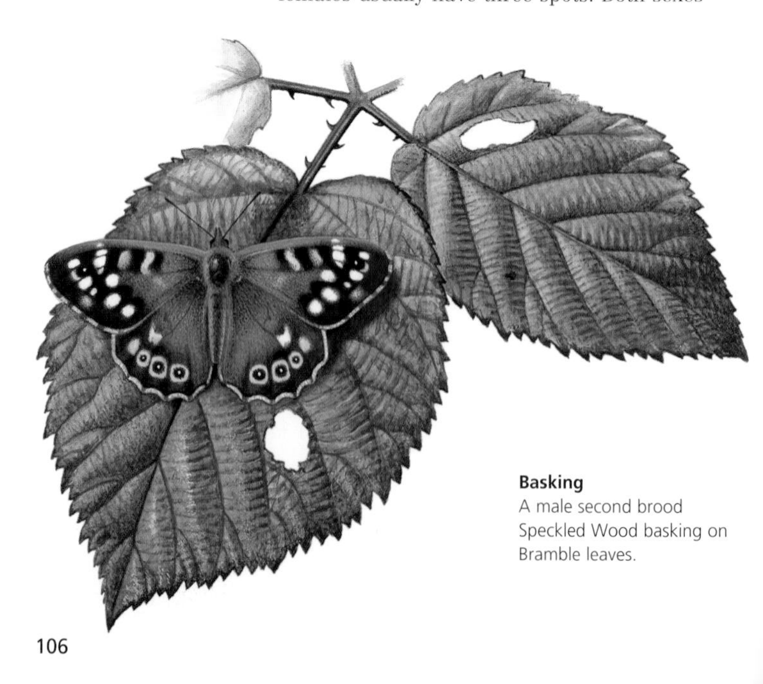

Basking
A male second brood Speckled Wood basking on Bramble leaves.

occasionally visit flowers late in the season, but prefer aphid honeydew from leaves in the woodland canopy.

Uniquely among our butterflies, the Speckled Wood can overwinter either as a caterpillar or a chrysalis, giving rise to up to three overlapping broods that first appear in late March and continue until mid-October.

Adult
The pale spots of the female are larger than those of the male, and both sexes of later broods are darker than those of the first. Various subspecies occur throughout Britain and Ireland. Those from the north have paler markings, while in the south they are more orange.

× 15

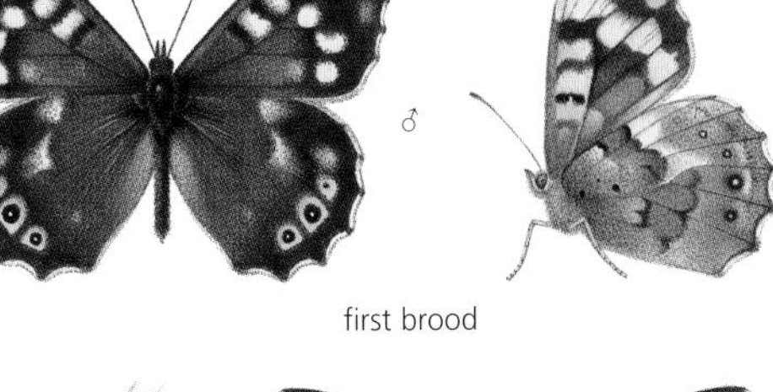

first brood

Egg
Eggs are laid singly on a wide range of grasses, including False Brome, Cock's-foot and Yorkshire-fog, growing in warm sheltered places. They hatch after ten days.

× 2.25

first brood

Chrysalis
The chrysalis may be bright green or dark olive, and hangs from a grass blade or concealed among vegetation.

Caterpillar
The caterpillars of later broods are unusual in that they can either hibernate or change into a chrysalis. Those that hibernate remain as caterpillars for six to eight months, the others for one month.

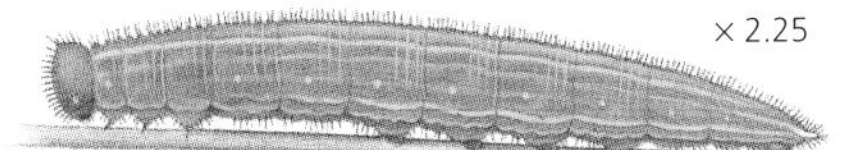

× 2.25

	JAN	FEB	MAR	APR	MAY	JUN	JUL	AUG	SEP	OCT	NOV	DEC
EGG												
CATERPILLAR												
CHRYSALIS												
ADULT												

Wall

Lasiommata megera

Throughout the last century the Wall has fluctuated in abundance, and in recent decades it has become quite scarce in central and southern England. In coastal areas, however, where the climate is milder and drier, populations have fared better, and there has been a slight northward expansion. This is a butterfly that loves hot, sun-baked places, where the ground is dry and broken. Disused railway lines, field edges, coastal dunes and rabbit-grazed downland are all frequented.

Most males spend much of their time patrolling their territories and basking alertly on the ground. The female, too, enjoys sunbathing and visiting flowers, but is less conspicuous when egg-laying. Two broods are normally produced, the first from late April until late June, and the second from mid-July until mid-September, although in the north they appear

Basking
A male Wall basking on hot stony ground.

up to two weeks later. In hot summers, a third brood sometimes flies in late September and October.

The bright markings of the Wall could sometimes cause it to be mistaken for a fritillary, but its rapid dancing flight, interspersed with glides and rests on the ground, is characteristic.

Adult
The female is larger and brighter and lacks the male's conspicuous black sex brand across the forewings. The intricate markings on the undersides of both sexes are beautifully cryptic when at rest.

× 15

Egg
The eggs are laid singly on the blades of various grasses growing in warm, sheltered places, including Cock's-foot, Tor-grass, Wavy Hair-grass and Yorkshire-fog. They hatch after ten days.

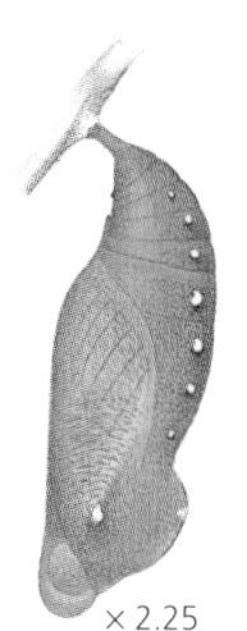
× 2.25

Chrysalis
Suspended among grass stems, the chrysalis varies from bright green to black. The adult butterfly emerges after two weeks.

Caterpillar
Caterpillars from the second brood overwinter, feeding occasionally in mild weather. They remain as caterpillars for about six months, while those from the first brood spend five weeks in this stage.

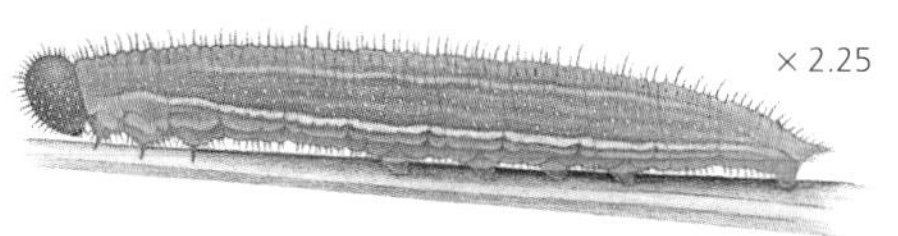
× 2.25

	JAN	FEB	MAR	APR	MAY	JUN	JUL	AUG	SEP	OCT	NOV	DEC
EGG												
CATERPILLAR												
CHRYSALIS												
ADULT												

Mountain Ringlet

Erebia epiphron

Our only true montane butterfly, the Mountain Ringlet is found on grassy mountain slopes in the Lake District and the Scottish Highlands. It flies in bright sunshine only, and although some colonies may contain thousands of individuals, in cool weather they disappear into the grasses and may be passed by unnoticed. Numbers in both areas appear stable and it is likely, as colonies are tight-knit and in remote habitats, that many more colonies are yet to be found.

Only one brood occurs, in the Lake District from mid-June until late July, and in Scotland from early July until early August. The male appears first and is by far the more conspicuous sex, with many often being seen, zig-zagging low over damp grassland, avoiding strong winds and tenaciously investigating any object that could be a female. The female, on the other hand, seldom flies, being weighed down by her heavy load of eggs. Both males and females will sometimes feed from flowers they encounter, but as adult butterflies only live for a few days, large nectar supplies are not essential.

This small, dark butterfly is unlikely to be confused with

Feeding
A female Mountain Ringlet feeding from Tormentil.

any other. The Scotch Argus is a close relative but is larger, more brightly marked with eye-spots and is usually found at lower altitudes than the Mountain Ringlet.

Overgrazing and the planting of conifers have reduced some populations, but it remains to be seen if climate change will push the species' distribution further north.

Adult

The female is larger, with a plumper abdomen, her wings are slightly paler and the orange bands are broader than those of the male. Scottish specimens tend to be altogether bigger and brighter.

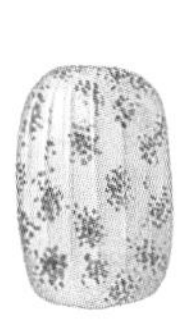

× 15

♂

Egg

The large eggs are laid singly on a blade of Mat-grass. Yellow at first, they develop reddish blotches after four days, and hatch in two to three weeks.

♀

♂

Lake District form

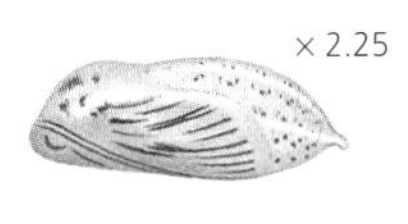

× 2.25

Chrysalis

The chrysalis is formed in a frail silken shelter, where it remains for about three weeks.

Caterpillar

The young caterpillar enters hibernation in September and re-emerges the following spring. It feeds sluggishly by night and is fully grown in May, living in total for about ten months. Occasionally individuals overwinter twice.

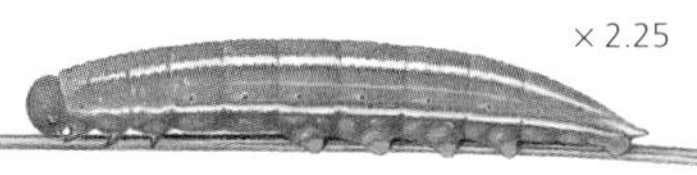

× 2.25

	JAN	FEB	MAR	APR	MAY	JUN	JUL	AUG	SEP	OCT	NOV	DEC
EGG												
CATERPILLAR												
CHRYSALIS												
ADULT												

Scotch Argus

Erebia aethiops

The Scotch Argus is widespread and common throughout much of Scotland, especially in the Highlands and along the west coast, where some colonies can be enormous. In England it is reduced to only two localities, and is declining generally throughout Europe. It occurs from sea level up to 500m, and in Scotland it flies in damp grassy areas, sheltered valleys, bogs and woodland edges. The English populations are found on scrubby limestone grassland dominated by Blue Moor-grass.

The male sometimes flies on mild overcast days, but this sun-loving insect prefers warm sunshine, and in the right conditions males appear abundantly, flying low and erratically over grassland, searching for females. After mating, the female spends time basking in the sun and supping nectar from Brambles and a variety of other flowers, flying reluctantly to lay her eggs in sunny spots where tall grasses grow. Only one brood appears, flying from late July until early September, with peak numbers in early August.

It is not known why the Scotch Argus has disappeared from many places, especially in the south of its range, but it is intolerant of heavy grazing and the planting of

Basking
The female Scotch Argus spends much of her life basking in the sunshine.

dense stands of conifers. Fortunately, the two English colonies are thriving, but it is strange that suitable habitat nearby has not been successfully colonised.

The dark, almost black appearance of the Scotch Argus distinguishes it from all other butterflies. The smaller Mountain Ringlet flies at higher altitudes.

Adult

The female is slightly paler, with broader orange bands and larger eye-spots. The width of the orange band varies, with some individuals occasionally having greatly enlarged eye-spots.

× 15

♂

Egg

Pale yellow when first laid, the large eggs develop darker speckles after a few days. They are laid singly on Purple Moor-grass in Scotland and on Blue Moor-grass in northern England. They hatch after two weeks.

× 15

♀

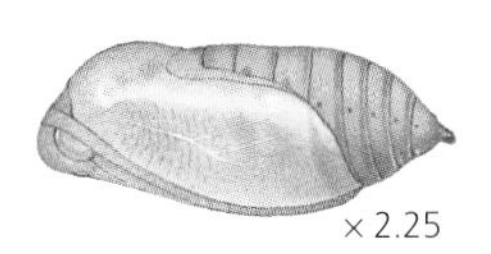

× 2.25

Chrysalis

The chrysalis is formed in a light cocoon at the base of the foodplant, where it remains concealed for two to three weeks.

♀

Caterpillar

After hatching the caterpillar feeds for a month, then enters hibernation in a grass tussock until the following spring, when it continues feeding, mainly at night, until early July.

× 2.25

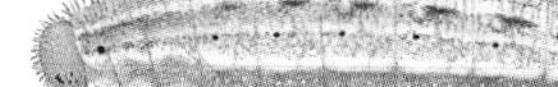

JAN FEB MAR APR MAY JUN JUL AUG SEP OCT NOV DEC

EGG
CATERPILLAR
CHRYSALIS
ADULT

Marbled White

Melanargia galathea

The unmistakable Marbled White is a lovely butterfly of unimproved flowery grassland. It has spread northwards and eastwards in recent years and has also been successfully introduced into some sites. It thrives following hot, dry summers, and despite the destruction of many flower-rich meadows it has spread to diverse habitats such as disused railway lines, roadside verges and waste ground. It also does well along rough woodland rides and coastal paths, and on chalk downland.

Many colonies, particularly in the south, contain thousands of butterflies, and in good years individuals disperse and may be seen wandering far from their breeding sites. Normally, though, this is a sedentary butterfly that spends most sunny days flapping lazily in the sun, feeding and basking on knapweeds and scabiouses, in company with skipper and blue butterflies. However, sometimes in extreme heat, in dull weather and at dusk, several Marbled Whites may be found roosting together on flowerheads, with their wings held tightly shut. The short flight period is from mid-June until mid-August, in a single brood.

Feeding
Female Marbled Whites feeding from Common Knapweed, a favourite nectar source.

Egg

The female lays or drops her large eggs randomly as she flutters among vegetation where Sheep's-fescue, Red Fescue or Tor-grass grow. They fall to the ground and hatch after three weeks.

♀

Adult

The upperside of the female is greyer than that of the male, and the front edge of the forewings and the underside of the hindwings are more ochreous. The pale ground colour and the extent of the black markings vary, with rare near-black aberrations sometimes occurring.

Caterpillar

Immediately after emerging, the young caterpillar enters hibernation in a grassy tussock. It reappears in the spring and feeds by day when small and at night when it gets bigger. The caterpillar stage lasts for about 11 months until pupation around June.

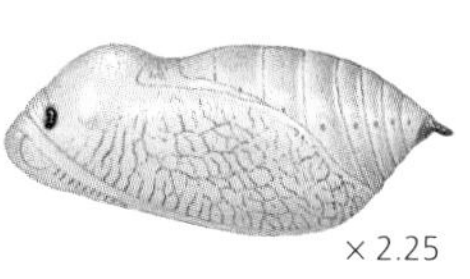

Chrysalis

Concealed on the ground beneath grass tussocks, the chrysalis stage lasts for two to three weeks.

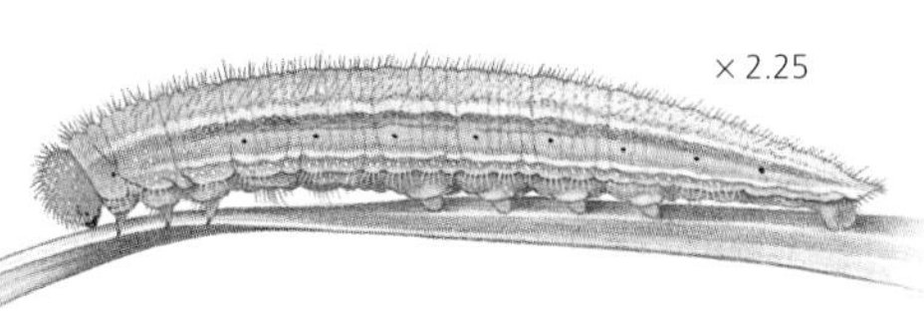

JAN FEB MAR APR MAY JUN JUL AUG SEP OCT NOV DEC

EGG
CATERPILLAR
CHRYSALIS
ADULT

Graylings fly late in the year, first appearing in early July and continuing in a single brood until mid-September. A unique population occurs on Great Ormes Head, in north Wales, where they are smaller and appear several weeks earlier.

Grayling

Hipparchia semele

Of all our butterflies, the Grayling offers the best example of cryptic camouflage, blending perfectly with its background when it is at rest. Its distribution is mainly coastal and it occurs in many habitats and soil types, from acidic heaths to chalk and limestone downs, cliffs and old quarries. Inland, thinly-wooded lowland heaths are its main haunts, but wherever it is found the soil is always well drained and baked dry by the sun. It lives in colonies, some of which on the southern heaths of England contain many thousands of butterflies.

The Grayling is often encountered when disturbed from the ground. It flies rapidly with a distinctive bobbing and gliding flight, sometimes dropping suddenly to the ground, disappearing from view. When it settles it tilts itself towards or faces the sun head on, to regulate its temperature. After an elaborate courtship involving the male stroking the female's antennae between his wings, the female sets about egg-laying, seeking small tussocks of grass growing in warm, sheltered hollows.

Resting
The cryptically patterned markings of the Grayling camouflage it at rest.

Egg
The eggs are laid singly on blades of various grasses, such as Sheep's-fescue, Bristle Bent and Tufted Hair-grass, growing in warm sheltered places. They hatch after two to three weeks.

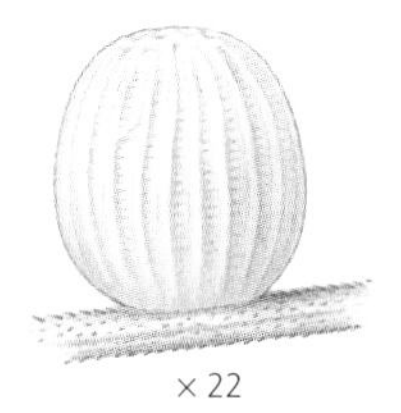
× 22

Chrysalis
Pupation takes place just below ground level in an earthen cell lined with silk, where the chrysalis remains for about a month.

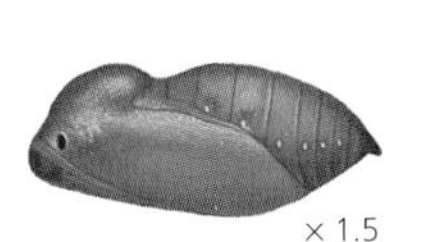
× 1.5

Adult
The female is larger and more brightly marked with orange, which can only be seen in flight as Graylings always settle with their wings closed. The undersides of both sexes are similar, but can vary from chalky to almost black, according to the surrounding soil type.

Caterpillar
This stage lasts for ten months. The nocturnal caterpillar hibernates when small but feeds occasionally on mild winter days. The following spring it resumes feeding, hiding by day, camouflaged at the base of a grass tussock.

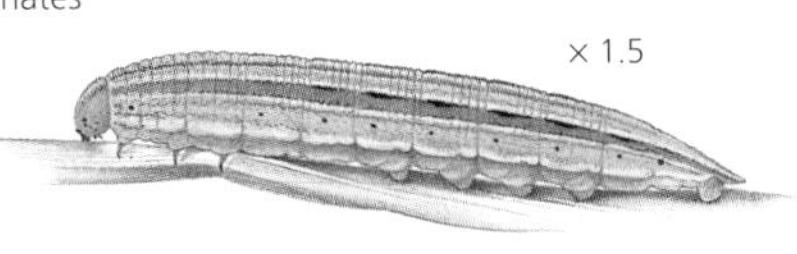
× 1.5

JAN FEB MAR APR MAY JUN JUL AUG SEP OCT NOV DEC

EGG
CATERPILLAR
CHRYSALIS
ADULT

Found as far north as Cumbria and Yorkshire, in the past 30 years populations of the Gatekeeper have increased and the species' range has expanded, with several new colonies being established in urban areas.

Gatekeeper

Pyronia tithonus

The Gatekeeper is also known as the Hedge Brown, and as both names suggest, this attractive little butterfly frequents lanes and hedgerows broken by sunny gateways, edged with Brambles and long grasses. It is also found in open woodland rides, on sea cliffs, scrubby downland and heaths, providing there is shelter and an abundance of tall vegetation.

The dancing flight of the Gatekeeper is unhurried as it appears to hop along hedgerows or woodland rides. However, it is sedentary, seldom wandering far outside its colony, which may vary in size from a few dozen to many thousands of individuals in suitable habitats in the south. Both sexes love to bask in the sun with their wings spread, and to feed, jostling with each other on Brambles, ragworts and a variety of other

Feeding
Ragworts and other flowers with an open nectar source are visited in late summer.

flowers. Early Gatekeepers appear in late June and continue in a single brood until the end of August, with a few stragglers lasting into early September.

The Gatekeeper often feeds in company with the Meadow Brown, but can easily be distinguished as the latter is a larger, duller butterfly, with a single white pupil in the eye-spots of the forewings. The underside of the Gatekeeper is more richly coloured and has an uneven row of white points.

Adult

Although the undersides of the sexes are similar, the uppersides are distinct: the smaller male is deeper orange, with a broad dark sex brand across the forewings.

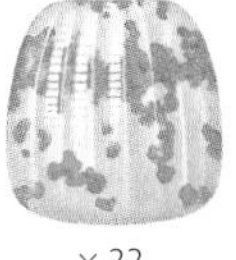

× 22

Egg

The eggs are laid or dropped among grasses, including Cock's-foot, meadow-grasses, Timothy, Common Couch and fescues. They hatch after three weeks.

× 2.25

Chrysalis

The chrysalis is suspended among vegetation near the ground. It may be pale green or ochreous with dark streaks, depending on its surroundings. The adult emerges after three weeks.

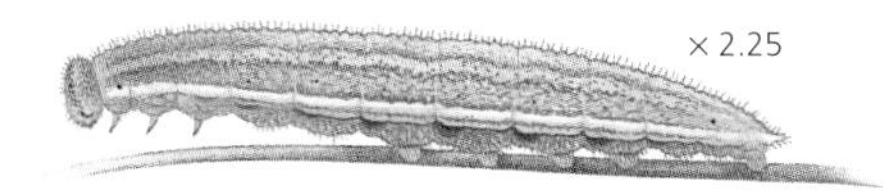

× 2.25

Caterpillar

The small caterpillar feeds in the daytime but in the spring, after hibernation, it starts feeding at night until it is fully grown at about nine months old. It may be pale green or ochreous.

	JAN	FEB	MAR	APR	MAY	JUN	JUL	AUG	SEP	OCT	NOV	DEC
EGG												
CATERPILLAR												
CHRYSALIS												
ADULT												

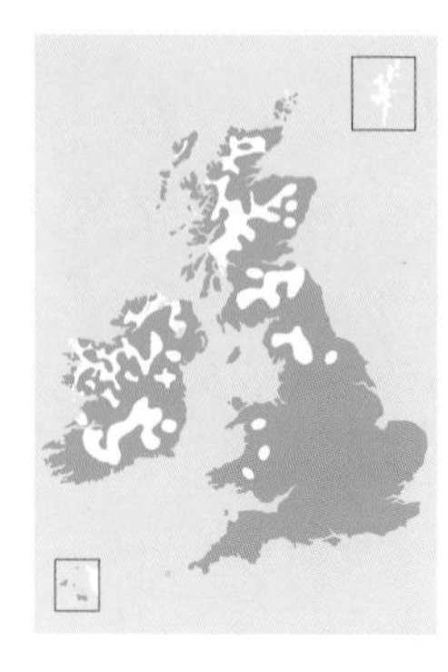

Meadow Brown

Maniola jurtina

Perhaps the commonest and most widespread of our butterflies, the Meadow Brown is found throughout Britain and Ireland, except for Shetland and hills above 300m. Populations are largest on the chalk downlands of southern England, where thousands of adults may fly. It is found in a wide range of habitats, including woodland rides, roadside verges, coastal dunes and urban wasteland. However, agricultural intensification has reduced its numbers in many areas.

The Meadow Brown has a long flight period, the first males appearing in late May in a single brood, often lasting into October. It is one of the few butterflies capable of flying on overcast days, but warm weather is preferred, when males spend much of their time searching for females and visiting flowers growing among tall, wild grasses. The female is more sedentary and often rests camouflaged on the ground. The markings on the underside of the hindwings have been the subject of much research into evolutionary genetics, with certain forms occurring in

Feeding
Both sexes can often be seen feeding from Bramble flowers.

particular habitats and behaving differently from other forms.

Other members of the 'browns', particularly the Gatekeeper, Ringlet and Marbled White, often occur with the Meadow Brown.

Adult

The sexes are distinct, but the amount of orange on both is variable, with races from the north and west being brighter, with much bolder eye-spots. The small black dots on the underside of the hindwings vary and may be absent.

Egg

The small eggs are yellow at first and develop reddish blotches after a week. They are laid, or dropped, among grasses, including fescues, meadow-grasses, bents and rye-grasses. Depending on the temperature, they hatch in two to four weeks.

× 22

Chrysalis

Firmly suspended low down on a grass stem, the chrysalis may be plain green or striated with black. The adult emerges in about a month.

× 2.25

Caterpillar

After hibernation, the caterpillar feeds at night, when it is easy to find. It is always green and is hairier than other 'brown' caterpillars. Many are slow to mature, giving rise to adults emerging late in the flight period.

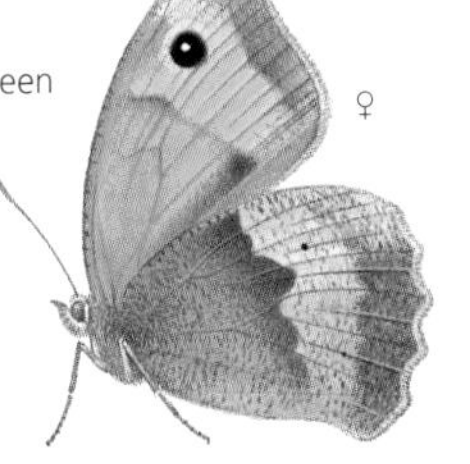

× 2.25

	JAN	FEB	MAR	APR	MAY	JUN	JUL	AUG	SEP	OCT	NOV	DEC
EGG												
CATERPILLAR												
CHRYSALIS												
ADULT												

Ringlet

Aphantopus hyperantus

This unassuming butterfly, whose past fortunes have fluctuated, is now quite common and widely distributed in many places throughout Britain and Ireland, although, curiously, it is absent from parts of Scotland and north-west England. Its range has expanded in recent decades and it has even recolonised some suburban areas, where pollution had been blamed for its absence.

The Ringlet is found mainly in damp woodland glades, along shady hedgerows and on riverbanks, often on heavy soil where the vegetation is lush. It also occurs in more open places, such as scrubby downland, especially further north, but avoids hot, dry habitats and suffers seriously following drought years. Males appear first in mid-June, and the single brood continues until mid-August. Ringlets spend most summer days in search of mates and feeding from a variety of flowers; they will also fly in dull or even drizzly weather.

When fresh, the dark

Feeding
Ringlets feed and rest on shrubs such as Wild Privet on downland sites.

velvety wings with their conspicuous white borders are distinctive, as is the unique underside, but specimens soon fade and some can resemble male Meadow Browns. However, even in flight there is no trace of orange and the eye-spots of the Ringlet can be clearly seen as it flops along a woodland ride.

Adult
Males tend to be smaller and darker than females, often with hardly any markings on the uppersides. The undersides are subject to extreme variation, with eye-spots either virtually absent, or large and distorted.

Egg
The eggs are dropped among lush growths of coarse grasses, including Cock's-foot, False Brome, Tor-grass and Tufted Hair-grass. They hatch after 18 days.

× 22

Chrysalis
Formed on the ground in a loose silken cocoon, the chrysalis lasts for about two weeks.

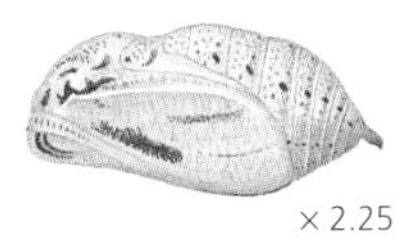
× 2.25

Caterpillar
The sluggish caterpillar feeds occasionally on mild winter evenings but fully resumes its nocturnal feeding in the spring. It is fully grown in June, when it is ten months old.

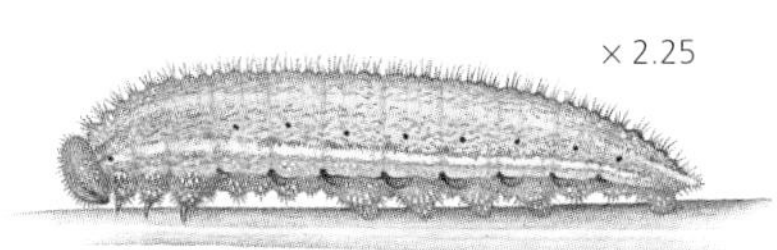
× 2.25

JAN FEB MAR APR MAY JUN JUL AUG SEP OCT NOV DEC

EGG
CATERPILLAR
CHRYSALIS
ADULT

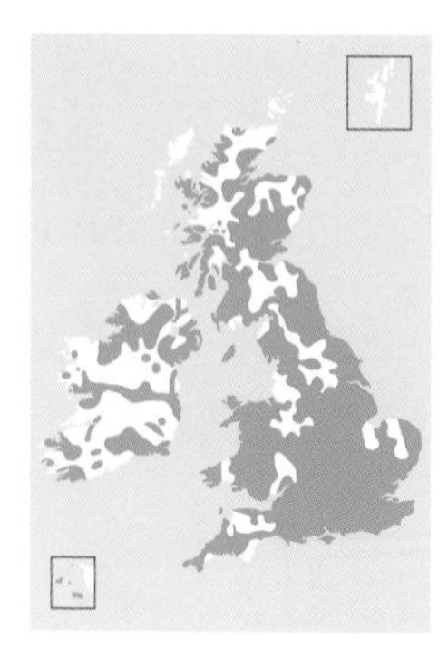

Small Heath

Coenonympha pamphilus

This inconspicuous little insect is one of our commonest grassland butterflies, but it has declined slightly in recent decades, as flowery meadows and uncultivated downland have been destroyed or fertilised. The Small Heath has a preference for dry, light soils where a mix of fine grasses grow, on downs, heaths, cliffs and even mountain slopes, although smaller colonies may be found on heavier soils.

The number of broods varies from one in northern Britain to up to three in the south, the first butterflies appearing in early May, with overlapping broods lasting until October. Males group together in territories to await passing females. After mating they go their separate ways, the female wandering in search of suitable egg-laying sites. Both sexes visit a wide variety of wild flowers, and spend much of their time weakly fluttering close to the ground, always settling with their wings firmly closed.

The closely-related Large Heath is found in wetter habitats than the Small Heath. It is generally bigger, duskier and more heavily spotted on the underside, although the Scottish race can look very similar. This is, however, the largest race, and apart from its size the main

Feeding
The wings of the Small Heath are always held shut when feeding.

distinguishing feature is the pale margin to the upperside of the wings. On the underside of the hindwings, which are easier to study, the pale mark is more sharply pointed towards the margin. At rest, the Small Heath is well camouflaged, but its weak, erratic flight is conspicuous and may more closely resemble some of the day-flying geometrid moths.

Adult
The female is usually rather larger and paler than the male, but the ground colour and the size of the spots are variable in both sexes. Specimens from western Scotland may be duller than those from the south.

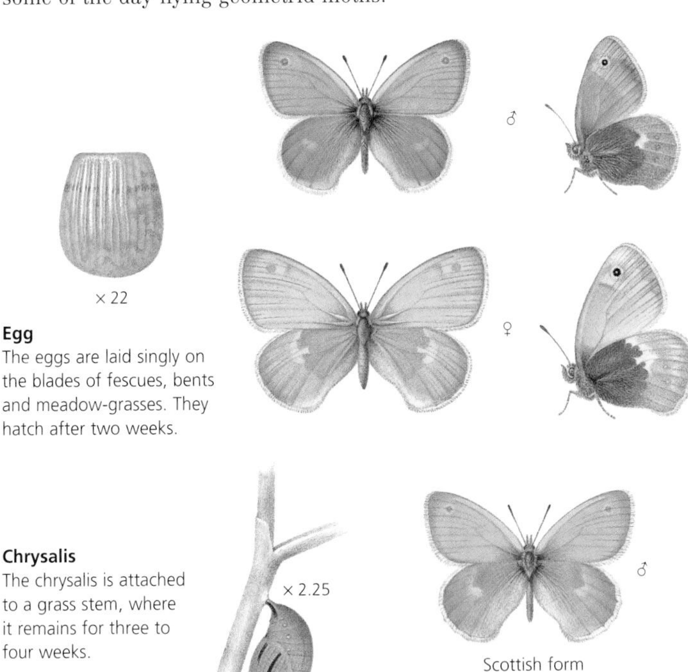

Scottish form

Egg
The eggs are laid singly on the blades of fescues, bents and meadow-grasses. They hatch after two weeks.

Chrysalis
The chrysalis is attached to a grass stem, where it remains for three to four weeks.

× 2.25

Caterpillar
Hibernation takes place at various stages of growth, and in the spring the larger caterpillars are ready to pupate. They feed mainly at night, and are beautifully concealed among fine grasses. Those that overwinter live for about ten months.

JAN FEB MAR APR MAY JUN JUL AUG SEP OCT NOV DEC
EGG
CATERPILLAR
CHRYSALIS
ADULT

Large Heath

Coenonympha tullia

Restricted to open, swampy moors and heaths of northern Britain and Ireland, the Large Heath is a sedentary butterfly that lives in self-contained colonies, some of which, particularly those in northern Scotland, may contain many thousands of individuals. It becomes increasingly scarce in the south of its range, in north Wales and northern England, where many colonies have been lost as a result of drainage, peat extraction and the afforestation of its habitats. Its future in many places, therefore, depends on the preservation of lowland raised bogs and acidic moorland.

The Large Heath is single-brooded and first appears in mid-June. Individuals only live for a few days, but the flight period lasts until early August, although further north emergence may be up to a month later. Its flight, like that of the Small Heath, is restless and erratic, keeping low to the ground. While on warm, sunny days it is fond of visiting flowers such as Cross-leaved Heath, it is also active in overcast weather.

Three named forms occur, ranging from the darker, more heavily spotted form in the south (*davus*) to the pale, plain form (*scotica*) in the far north. Between these two populations, the form *polydama* occurs. It is suggested that the heavily spotted forms in the warmer south are more active, and have evolved the spots to tempt birds to peck at these 'eyes' rather than at their bodies.

Feeding
The Large Heath's most favoured nectar source is Cross-leaved Heath.

form *davus*

Adult

The sexes are difficult to tell apart at rest as the Large Heath always settles with its wings shut. Although there is much variation between the races, aberrations are rare.

Egg

The large eggs are laid singly on a dried stem at the base of a tussock of Hare's-tail Cottongrass or less often of Common Cottongrass. They hatch after two weeks.

× 22

form *davus*

× 2.25

form *scotica*

Chrysalis

Similar to but straighter than that of the Small Heath, it is suspended among grasses for three weeks.

Caterpillar

The caterpillar lives and hibernates in dense grass tussocks. It emerges in the spring and continues feeding until June, when it is about ten months old. Some caterpillars overwinter twice.

form *polydama*

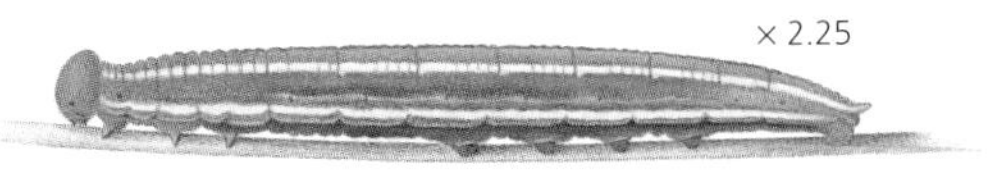

× 2.25

	JAN	FEB	MAR	APR	MAY	JUN	JUL	AUG	SEP	OCT	NOV	DEC
EGG												
CATERPILLAR												
CHRYSALIS												
ADULT												

Extinct species and rare migrants

Pale Clouded Yellow

Colias hyale

This rare migrant butterfly and the very similar Berger's Clouded Yellow arrive from the Mediterranean into southern Britain in very small numbers, with most reports coming from Kent, Essex and Sussex. Its flight is fast and powerful and it is most likely to be seen dashing across fields where clovers and Lucerne, the caterpillar's foodplants, grow in abundance. The first arrivals are in May and June; the resulting offspring of these migrants fly in August and September. However, caterpillars produced from this generation fail to survive our damp winters.

It is extremely difficult to tell the Pale and Berger's Clouded Yellows apart, especially the females. The former has slightly more pointed forewings with straighter outer margins, and the ground colour of the male is pale greenish yellow. Also, the dark basal dusting near the body and the markings around the edge of the hindwings are heavier. The white female, form *helice*, of the Clouded Yellow (see page 33) has broader black margins and a much darker suffusion of grey on the hindwings, although this is difficult to see, as all *Colias* species sit with their wings closed. The caterpillars are the easiest stage of the life cycle in which to separate the Pale Clouded from the Berger's Clouded Yellow (see opposite).

× 1.5

Berger's Clouded Yellow

Colias alfacariensis

Even scarcer than the Pale Clouded Yellow, the Berger's Clouded Yellow was only recognised as a separate species as recently as 1947, although collections have shown that it occurred in Britain long before then, leading to much confusion over records. It is quicker on the wing, though less migratory than the Pale Clouded Yellow, and is more likely to be seen on downland, where its caterpillar feeds on Horseshoe Vetch. Its time of appearance and its life cycle are similar to that of its near relative, and it, too, is unlikely to survive our winters.

The main differences between the three *Colias* yellows are described opposite, but the most distinctive part of the Berger's Clouded Yellow's life cycle is its caterpillar, which is green, with two yellow lines with black spots below, running along each side, making it beautifully camouflaged among Horseshoe Vetch.

Black-veined White

Aporia crataegi

Despite several attempts to reintroduce the Black-veined White into Britain following its disappearance in the mid-1920s, it remains extinct and any occasional recent records are probably the result of captive releases, escapes or possibly immigration. Mainly southerly in its distribution, scattered colonies occurred as far north as Yorkshire, but it was a species whose numbers fluctuated from year to year, with occasional periods of abundance, particularly in the mid-19th century, when it was often the commonest butterfly on the wing.

Flying from late June until August, along overgrown hedgerows, woodland edges and flowery meadows, it was also found in orchards, where its larval webs occurred on apple and plum trees, as well as on hawthorns and Blackthorn in hedgerows.

The Black-veined White's flight is powerful, and although it bears a resemblance to other whites, its clear black veins are distinctive, especially when at rest. The reason for its demise is unclear, but it seems unlikely that the Black-veined White will become re-established in Britain.

Bath White

Pontia daplidice

In mainland Europe the Bath White is a common butterfly of flowery meadows and waysides, but in the British Isles it is a rare visitor that was prized by early butterfly collectors. Indeed, the world's oldest pinned butterfly – a Bath White – has just had its 300th birthday at Oxford University Museum.

The Bath White is an active wanderer with a rapid, purposeful flight, and is most likely to be seen in July and August. In recent decades only a few individuals have been recorded, and the last big influx was over 50 years ago. Eggs are laid on mignonettes and other crucifers, but in Britain caterpillars appearing in late summer inevitably perish.

Owing to its similarity to other whites, including the female Orange-tip, it is probable that Bath Whites have passed by unrecognised. However, at rest or during the female's fluttering egg-laying flight the attractive green mottling on the underside of the hindwings is distinctive, as is the large central spot on the forewings and the black markings, which are heavier in the female than in the male.

Long-tailed Blue

Lampides boeticus

Although a few individuals are recorded in southern England in most years, the Long-tailed Blue, which is continuously brooded in southern Europe, is incapable of surviving British winters in any stage of its life cycle. As well as genuine vagrants, which are mostly seen on chalk downland between June and October, some arrive as caterpillars from Africa, hidden in the pods of imported mangetout peas destined for the dinner plate.

This is a sun-loving little butterfly, with a quick, jerky flight. Both sexes are fond of flowers, and females may visit gardens to lay their eggs on the flower buds of Everlasting-pea, Bladder-senna and Broom.

In flight the Long-tailed Blue could easily be mistaken for a Common Blue, but when feeding or resting the intricate patterning and conspicuous broad white band on the underside, together with the hindwing 'tails', are diagnostic.

Short-tailed Blue

Cupido argiades

This diminutive little blue has never been known to breed in Britain and has been recorded on fewer than two dozen occasions. It was first captured in Dorset in 1885 and was then named the Bloxworth Blue. It is not a strong migrant and seldom crosses the English Channel. However, its range in Europe has been steadily expanding northwards and it is possible that global warming may affect its future occurrence in Britain. In mainland Europe it is a butterfly of scrubby grasslands and heaths, where Common Bird's-foot-trefoil, Red Clover, vetches, gorse and other caterpillar foodplants grow.

Most records are from between July and September, but in France it flies from April onwards, in several broods.

The violet-blue of the male is fairly constant but the amount of blue varies in the female, and she in particular could be mistaken for several of the commoner blues, notably the Small and Silver-studded. However, a close look at the underside shows a silvery-blue ground colour with conspicuous orange and black spots.

Mazarine Blue

Polyommatus semiargus

The last genuinely British Mazarine Blues died out at the end of the 19th century, although a few irregular records from as far north as Yorkshire continued into the early 1900s. Despite records from around two dozen English and Welsh counties, the main established localities were in Glamorgan, Gloucestershire and Dorset, the latter producing the largest number of records, with the species being regarded as quite common in some years.

In mainland Europe it occurs mainly in June and July, and flies in damp hay meadows with an abundance of Red Clover, the caterpillar's main foodplant. It has been suggested that the cultivation of this crop in England hastened the extinction of the Mazarine Blue, as it attracted females to lay their eggs on the crops and the eggs were then destroyed during harvesting.

It is not strongly migratory and in mainland Europe it has become scarcer in the north, so it seems unlikely, apart from an occasional vagrant, that the Mazarine Blue will become re-established here.

The deep blue of the male is distinctive but the undersides of both sexes, which resemble a large Small Blue, are the best means of confirming identification.

Geranium Bronze

Cacyreus marshalli

The most recent and dubious addition to the British butterfly list, the Geranium Bronze was first recorded in 1997 when two adults were seen in East Sussex. These were undoubtedly the result of their early stages having been accidentally imported with cultivated geraniums, hence the name. Since then, a few individuals appeared the following year, with singletons in Hampshire in 2000 and in Cambridgeshire in 2001. A resident of South Africa, the Geranium Bronze has spread northwards and has become an established pest in warm parts of southern Europe, where geraniums can survive the winter and where it can breed continuously without hibernating.

Despite nationwide publicity in the media and panic among Pelargonium growers, the predicted demise of the cultivated geranium has not happened, and it seems that unless the greenhouse effect happens literally, the Geranium Bronze will have to rely on importation and heated glasshouses for its occasional appearances in Britain.

It has a weak flight, fluttering around and basking on geranium plants, when the hindwing tails and the distinctive contrast between the plain upperside and intricate underside make identification easy.

Large Copper

Lycaena dispar

The English subspecies of the brilliant Large Copper became extinct about 150 years ago, a little over 100 years after it was first discovered in 1749. Its rarity and beauty made it highly prized among butterfly collectors and many thousands of adults and caterpillars were collected. However, it was not over-collecting which led to its demise but the extensive drainage of the vast fenlands of East Anglia. This was its main stronghold, although it was once more widely distributed, and occurred in the Somerset Levels and the Wye marshes in Monmouthshire.

About a dozen attempts at reintroduction were made during the last century, using the similar Dutch race *batavus*. The most successful of these was the Woodwalton Fen population, in Huntingdonshire, which survived from 1927 until 1994 when it finally died out, despite its numbers being constantly boosted by captive-bred reinforcements. Recent research and the restoration of suitable broadland habitats in Norfolk may warrant further attempts at reintroduction in the future.

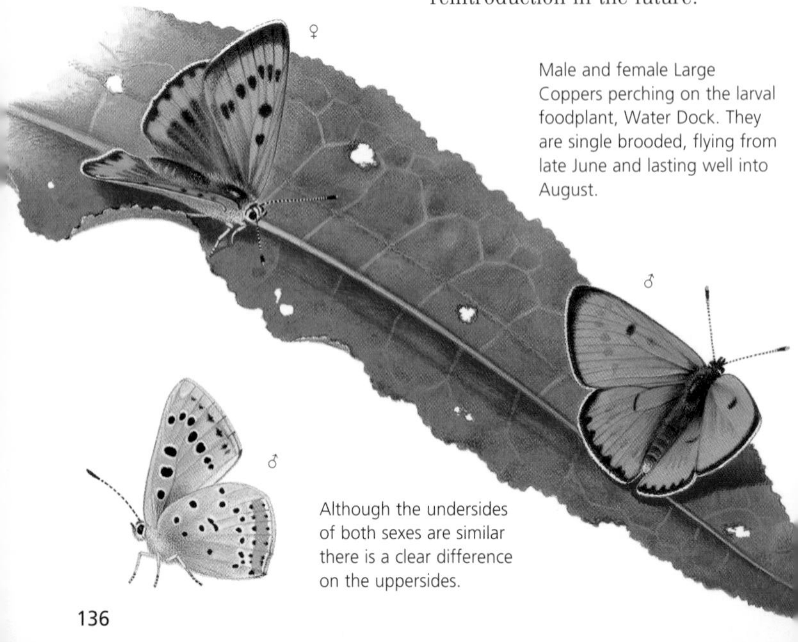

Male and female Large Coppers perching on the larval foodplant, Water Dock. They are single brooded, flying from late June and lasting well into August.

Although the undersides of both sexes are similar there is a clear difference on the uppersides.

Queen of Spain Fritillary

Issoria lathonia

One of the commonest and most widespread of the European fritillaries, the beautiful Queen of Spain Fritillary is a rare visitor to Britain. A colony was thought to have become established briefly in Suffolk during the late 1990s. Since then, there have been few records, but with populations just across the English Channel, and with climate change, it could become a more frequent visitor.

This strong-flying butterfly, which is found in open uncultivated places, heaths and flowery meadows containing Wild Pansy, spends much of its time on the ground, basking in the sun. It flies from June onwards but most records are from September and October, these late specimens possibly being the offspring of earlier immigrants. It is thought that overwintering can take place in the caterpillar, chrysalis or adult stage.

Fritillaries are difficult to tell apart in flight, but at rest the uniform black spots and elegantly curved forewings of the Queen of Spain Fritillary are unique, as are the silver spots on the underside, which are bolder than those of any other European fritillary.

Large Tortoiseshell

Nymphalis polychloros

Once generally distributed throughout England and Wales, the Large Tortoiseshell is now thought to be extinct, and of the few specimens that are occasionally recorded, most are probably captive-bred releases. It has always been a butterfly whose numbers have fluctuated greatly, but it is now more than 50 years since it appeared in large numbers and it seems unlikely the species will ever recover.

A butterfly of woodland edges and hedgerows that abound in elms, willows and poplars, it was already a rarity when Dutch Elm Disease appeared; this could only have worsened its plight. The Large Tortoiseshell is first seen in spring, after hibernating in hollow trees and log piles. A single brood is then produced which is on the wing in July and August. It is a powerful flyer that visits a variety of flowers, but it especially likes the sap that oozes from tree wounds.

Although it is most closely related to the Camberwell Beauty, it looks more like the commoner Small Tortoiseshell, but the latter is brighter, with a white spot near the apex of the forewing, and has more contrast on the undersides.

Camberwell Beauty

Nymphalis antiopa

Named after Camberwell in south-east London, where the first two specimens were seen in 1748, most sightings of the beautiful Camberwell Beauty now are from eastern England, between August and October. However, in good years, when large numbers of immigrants appear from Scandinavia, records may come from throughout Britain and Ireland. The most recent of these influxes, known as '*antiopa* years', were in 1976 and 1995, and in the latter year there were more than 350 sightings.

In mainland Europe the Camberwell Beauty is found mainly in open woodlands where willows, elms and poplars grow, but it is a wanderer and when it arrives in Britain it may be found almost anywhere, although it has never been recorded as having bred here.

Like others in its family, the Camberwell Beauty visits a variety of flowers, sap weeping from trees and rotting fruit, and can then be easily approached. When it is basking in the sun, it is quickly alarmed and takes flight. It hibernates in log piles and hollow trees, from October onwards. British winters are apparently too damp and mild for it, although there are a few accounts of successful overwintering.

Monarch

Danaus plexippus

This famous North American giant usually turns up in small numbers each year in south-west England and southern Ireland, when it catches the attention of birdwatchers searching for autumn migrants from the west. Although resident in the Canary Isles and Spain, it is thought our Monarchs arrive from across the Atlantic, having been blown off course during their southerly mass migration to Mexico, as their arrival coincides with that of migrant American birds.

Until 60 years ago, a total of about 100 Monarchs only had been recorded in Britain, but in recent years sightings have become much more frequent, notably in 1981, 1995 and 1999, when in the latter year over 300 were seen. Unfortunately, its larval foodplant, the toxic milkweed, is not native in Britain, so Monarchs are unable to lay their eggs. Adults, however, continue to live on until September and October, visiting flowers, including garden plants, usually near the coast.

Its strong, flapping flight, size and unmistakable coloration ensure the Monarch is easily identified, as it is unlike any other northern European butterfly.

Day-flying moths

Many species of moth fly by day, or may be disturbed from vegetation, often causing confusion in identification. Butterflies have a club at the tip of the antennae, whereas most day-flying moths can be distinguished from butterflies by their simple thread-like or feathered antennae. The conspicuous burnet moths have curved, slightly clubbed antennae. The species illustrated here are a small selection of some of the more colourful moths that may catch the eye, with an indication of their main habitats.

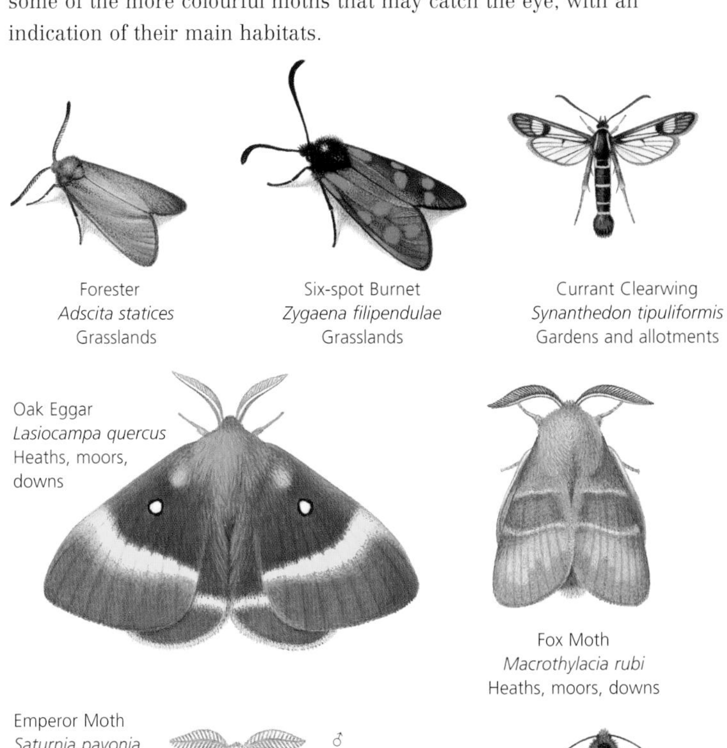

Forester
Adscita statices
Grasslands

Six-spot Burnet
Zygaena filipendulae
Grasslands

Currant Clearwing
Synanthedon tipuliformis
Gardens and allotments

Oak Eggar
Lasiocampa quercus
Heaths, moors, downs

Fox Moth
Macrothylacia rubi
Heaths, moors, downs

Emperor Moth
Saturnia pavonia
Heaths and moors

Orange Underwing
Archiearis parthenias
Birch woodland

Silver-ground Carpet
Xanthorhoe montanata
Damp places

Shaded Broad-bar
Scotopteryx chenopodiata
Grasslands

Lesser Treble-bar
Aplocera efformata
Grasslands and rides

Latticed Heath
Chiasmia clathrata
Grasslands and heaths

Brown Silver-line
Petrophora chlorosata
Bracken

Speckled Yellow
Pseudopanthera macularia
Open woodland

Common Heath
Ematurga atomaria
Heaths and moors

Yellow Belle
Semiaspilates ochrearia
Coasts

Broad-bordered Bee Hawkmoth
Hemaris fuciformis
Open woodland

Humming-bird Hawkmoth
Macroglossum stellatarum
Coasts to gardens

Vapourer
Orgyia antiqua
Widespread inc. gardens

Wood Tiger
Parasemia plantagini
Moors, heaths, dowr

Clouded Buff
Diacrisia sannio
Heaths, moors, downs

Scarlet Tiger
Callimorpha dominula
Fens and marshes

Cinnabar
Tyria jacobaeae
Dry grasslands and heaths

Dusky Sallow
Eremobia ochroleuca
Grasslands

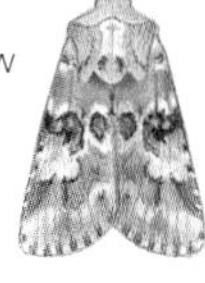

Beautiful Yellow Underwing
Anarta myrtilli
Heaths and moors

Silver Y
Autographa gamma
Widespread immigrant

Mother Shipton
Callistege mi
Grasslands

Burnet Companion
Euclidia glyphica
Grasslands

Small Purple-barred
Phytometra viridaria
Grasslands and heaths

Further reading

Asher, J, Warren, M, Fox, R, Harding, P, & Jeffcoate, S 2001 *The Millennium Atlas of Butterflies in Britain and Ireland.* Oxford University Press

Brooks, M, & Knight, C 1982 *A Complete Guide to British Butterflies.* Jonathan Cape

Dennis, R L H 1977 *British Butterflies, Their Origin and Establishment.* E W Classey

Emmet, A M, & Heath, J (eds) 1989 *The Moths and Butterflies of Great Britain and Ireland, Volume 7 Pt. 1: The Butterflies.* Harley Books

Thomas, J A, & Lewington, R 1991 *The Butterflies of Britain and Ireland.* Dorling Kindersley

Thompson, G 1980 *The Butterflies of Scotland.* Croom Helm

Index

Common names

Butterflies

Admiral, Red 80
  White 76
Argus, Brown 60
  Northern Brown 62
  Scotch 112
Blue
  Adonis 68
  Chalkhill 66
  Common 64
  Holly 70
  Large 72
  Long-tailed 132
  Mazarine 134
  Short-tailed 133
  Silver-studded 58
  Small 56
Brimstone 34
Camberwell Beauty 139
Comma 88
Copper, Large 136
  Small 54
Duke of Burgundy 74
Fritillary
  Dark Green 96
  Glanville 102
  Heath 104
  High Brown 94
  Marsh 100
  Pearl-bordered 92
  Queen of Spain 137
  Silver-washed 98
  Small Pearl-bordered 90
Gatekeeper 118
Geranium Bronze 135
Grayling 116
Hairstreak
  Black 52
  Brown 46
  Green 44
  Purple 48
  White-letter 50
Heath, Large 126
  Small 124
Meadow Brown 120
Monarch 140
Orange-tip 42
Painted Lady 82
Peacock 86
Purple Emperor 78
Ringlet 122
  Mountain 110
Skipper
  Chequered 12
  Dingy 24
  Essex 16
  Grizzled 26
  Large 22
  Lulworth 18
  Silver-spotted 20
  Small 14
Speckled Wood 106
Swallowtail 28
Tortoiseshell, Large 138
  Small 84
Wall 108
White
  Bath 131
  Black-veined 130
  Green-veined 40
  Large 36
  Marbled 114
  Real's Wood 30
  Small 38
  Wood 30
Yellow
  Berger's Clouded 129
  Clouded 32
  Pale Clouded 128

Moths

Beautiful Yellow Underwing 143
Broad-bordered Bee Hawkmoth 142
Brown Silver-line 142
Burnet Companion 143
Cinnabar 143
Clouded Buff 143
Common Heath 142
Currant Clearwing 141
Dusky Sallow 143
Emperor Moth 141
Forester 141
Fox Moth 141
Humming-bird Hawkmoth 142
Latticed Heath 142
Lesser Treble-bar 142
Mother Shipton 143
Oak Eggar 141
Orange Underwing 141
Scarlet Tiger 143
Shaded Broad-bar 142
Silver-ground Carpet 142
Silver Y 143
Six-spot Burnet 141
Small Purple-barred 143
Speckled Yellow 142
Vapourer 142
Wood Tiger 142
Yellow Belle 142

Scientific names

Adscita statices 141
Aglais urticae 84
Anarta myrtilli 143
Anthocharis cardamines 42
Apatura iris 78
Aphantopus hyperantus 122
Aplocera efformata 142
Aporia crataegi 130
Archiearis parthenias 141
Argynnis adippe 94
  aglaja 96
  paphia 98
Aricia agestis 60
  artaxerxes 62
Autographa gamma 143
Boloria euphrosyne 92
  selene 90
Cacyreus marshalli 135
Callimorpha dominula 143
Callistege mi 143
Callophrys rubi 44
Carterocephalus palaemon 12
Celastrina argiolus 70
Chiasmia clathrata 142
Coenonympha
  pamphilus 124
  tullia 126
Colias alfacariensis 129
  croceus 32
  hyale 128
Cupido argiades 133
  minimus 56
Danaus plexippus 140
Diacrisia sannio 143
Ematurga atomaria 142
Erebia aethiops 112
  epiphron 110
Eremobia ochroleuca 143
Erynnis tages 24
Euclidia glyphica 143
Euphydryas aurinia 100
Gonepteryx rhamni 34
Hamearis lucina 74
Hemaris fuciformis 142
Hesperia comma 20
Hipparchia semele 116
Inachis io 86
Issoria lathonia 137
Lampides boeticus 132
Lasiocampa quercus 141
Lasiommata megera 108
Leptidea reali 30
  sinapis 30
Limenitis camilla 76
Lycaena dispar 136
  phlaeas 54
Lysandra bellargus 68
  coridon 66
Macroglossum stellatarum 142
Macrothylacia rubi 141
Maculinea arion 72
Maniola jurtina 120
Melanargia galathea 114
Melitaea athalia 104
  cinxia 102
Neozephyrus quercus 48
Nymphalis antiopa 139
  polychloros 138
Ochlodes venata 22
Orgyia antiqua 142
Papilio machaon 28
Pararge aegeria 106
Parasemia plantaginis 142
Petrophora chlorosata 142
Phytometra viridaria 143
Pieris brassicae 36
  napi 40
  rapae 38
Plebeius argus 58
Polygonia c-album 88
Polyommatus icarus 64
  semiargus 134
Pontia daplidice 131
Pseudopanthera macularia 142
Pyrgus malvae 26
Pyronia tithonus 118
Saturnia pavonia 141
Satyrium pruni 52
  w-album 50
Scotopteryx chenopodiata 142
Semiaspilates ochrearia 142
Synanthedon tipuliformis 141
Thecla betulae 46
Thymelicus acteon 18
  lineola 16
  sylvestris 14
Tyria jacobaeae 143
Vanessa atalanta 80
  cardui 82
Xanthorhoe montanata 142
Zygaena filipendulae 141